COUNTRIES OF THE WORLD

Turkey

Gareth Stevens Publishing

A WORLD ALMANAC EDUCATION GROUP COMPANY

About the Authors: Born and raised in Australia, Neriman Kemal has a Turkish-Cypriot father, who sparked her passion for Turkey with stories of his homeland. Intrigued for years by the country's rich and colorful history and culture, Kemal moved to Turkey in her early twenties to teach English there. Today, she lives in Brisbane, Australia, and works as a freelance writer. Selina Kuo lives in Singapore and works as an editor. She studied journalism and English in Perth, Australia.

PICTURE CREDITS

Agence de Presse ANA: 22, 47, 73
Archive Photos: 13, 15 (bottom), 36, 37 (both), 75, 78 (top), 78 (bottom), 81, 83
Murat Atila: 85
Yaruz Atila: 84
Camera Press Ltd.: 15 (center), 45, 56, 60, 77
Haga Library, Japan: 30, 33 (top), 68, 69 (top)
Hulton Getty: 76 (both)
The Hutchison Library: 17, 46 (top), 50, 51, 64, 71
Images of Africa Photobank: 26
International Photobank: 2, 3 (bottom), 4, 6, 27, 31, 44, 48, 49, 57, 59, 91
John R. Jones: 9, 10, 23, 52
Nurten Karabulut: 82
Nazina Kowall: 3 (center), 8, 11, 21, 35, 39, 46 (bottom), 58, 62, 65, 70
North Wind Picture Archives: 12, 15 (top)
Christine Osborne Pictures: 28, 72
TEMA Foundation: 67
Topham Picturepoint: 16
Trip Photo Library: cover, 7, 14, 18, 19, 20 (bottom), 24, 25, 29, 32, 33 (bottom), 38, 40 (both), 41, 54, 55 (both), 61, 63, 66, 69 (bottom), 80
Nik Wheeler: 1, 3 (top), 5, 20 (top), 34, 42, 43, 53, 74, 79

Digital Scanning by Superskill Graphics Pte Ltd

Written by
NERIMAN KEMAL AND SELINA KUO

Edited by
SELINA KUO

Edited in the U.S. by
PATRICIA LANTIER
MONICA RAUSCH

Designed by
LYNN CHIN

Picture research by
SUSAN JANE MANUEL

First published in North America in 2001 by
Gareth Stevens Publishing
A World Almanac Education Group Company
330 West Olive Street, Suite 100
Milwaukee, Wisconsin 53212 USA

Please visit our web site at:
www.garethstevens.com
For a free color catalog describing
Gareth Stevens' list of high-quality books
and multimedia programs, call
1-800-542-2595 (USA) or
1-800-461-9120 (CANADA).
Gareth Stevens Publishing's
Fax: (414) 332-3567.

© **TIMES MEDIA PRIVATE LIMITED** 2001
Originated and designed by
Times Editions
An imprint of Times Media Private Limited
A member of the Times Publishing Group
Times Centre, 1 New Industrial Road
Singapore 536196
http://www.timesone.com.sg/te

Library of Congress Cataloging-in-Publication Data
Kemal, Neriman.
Turkey / by Neriman Kemal and Selina Kuo.
p. cm. — (Countries of the world)
Includes bibliographical references and index.
ISBN 0-8368-2341-9 (lib. bdg.)
1. Turkey — Juvenile literature. [1. Turkey] I. Kuo, Selina. II. Title.
III. Countries of the world (Milwaukee, Wis.)
DR417.4 .K46   2001
956.1—dc21   2001017031

Printed in Malaysia

1 2 3 4 5 6 7 8 9 05 04 03 02 01

Contents

4

AN OVERVIEW OF TURKEY

Modern Turkey, or the Republic of Turkey, was founded in 1923. A roughly rectangular area that lies between southeastern Europe and southwestern Asia, modern Turkey reflects the country's unique geographical position, adopting a mixture of Western and Eastern values into its society and culture. Before 1923, many great civilizations flourished in ancient Anatolia, the vast area encompassing Turkey today. One of the earliest empires was that of the Hittites in about 1900 B.C. The Persians, Greeks, Romans, and Seljuk Turks followed, and then the Ottomans ruled the area from 1326 until World War I. Since its independence, Turkey has struggled with issues of religion, Kurdish independence, and favorable relations with its neighbors and Western nations.

Opposite: **A crowd near the quay in Istanbul waits for fishing boats to dock. Turkey is rich in natural resources, including marine life.**

Below: **Kabob shops, such as these in Istanbul, are located throughout the country.**

THE FLAG OF TURKEY

The Turkish flag is red with a central design that consists of a white crescent and a white, five-pointed star. The format of the current Turkish flag was adopted in 1936. The origins of the design's symbols, however, date back to more distant times and are subject to much debate. The crescent was probably adopted by grateful citizens of Byzantium in 340, when an unusually bright moon emerged in the nick of time on a cloudy night to expose and foil an attack plotted by King Philip of Macedonia. The star is believed to have been added in 1459 by Ottoman Sultan Mehmet II, who believed in astrological symbols.

5

Geography

Diverse Landscapes

Turkey covers an area of 301,400 square miles (780,626 square kilometers) and is bordered by eight countries and three seas — the Black Sea to the north, Georgia and Armenia to the northeast, Azerbaijan and Iran to the east, Iraq and Syria to the southeast, the Mediterranean Sea and the Aegean Sea to the southwest and west, and Greece and Bulgaria to the northwest. Landscapes in Turkey vary greatly from the west to the east. The country spans about 1,000 miles (1,609 km) from end to end.

Western Turkey

Agriculture is widely practiced in northwestern and southwestern Turkey. The low hills and vast grasslands north of the Turkish Straits are used to cultivate grapes, peaches, and apricots, as well as raise livestock. Three major rivers — the Küçükmenderes, the Büyükmenderes, and the Gediz — sustain fertile plains and valleys in southwestern Turkey. The plains are home to olive and fig orchards, while tobacco is grown in the valleys.

THE TURKISH STRAITS

The Turkish Straits consist of the Bosporus, the Sea of Marmara, and the Dardanelles. Together, they form a crucial passageway of water in northwestern Turkey, providing the only link between the Black and Aegean seas.

Below: **Kalkan is a beautiful seaside town near the city of Dalaman in the province of Mugla.**

Central Turkey

The Anatolian Plateau is the area between the Pontic and Taurus mountains, stretching approximately from Bursa to Sivas. The plateau has highlands and scattered river valleys. The plateau's westernmost surface is especially uneven, with sections of upland and mountains that range from 1,500 to 6,500 feet (457 to 1,980 meters) in height. The southeastern section of the plateau has many volcanoes, including Mounts Hasan and Erciyes.

Eastern Turkey

Eastern Turkey is extremely mountainous. Along with the major mountain ranges, such as the Pontic and the Taurus mountains, as many as eleven mountain ranges are scattered throughout the region. Mount Ararat is the country's highest mountain at 16,950 feet (5,166 m). The Euphrates and the Tigris rivers flow from eastern Turkey into the Persian Gulf via Syria and Iraq. In Turkey, they flow for 776 miles (1,249 km) and 326 miles (525 km), respectively. Lake Van is Turkey's largest lake.

Above: The Tigris River, shown here flowing past the town of Hasankeyf in the province of Batman, merges with the Euphrates River in Iraq before emptying into the Persian Gulf.

EARTHQUAKES: THE NORTH ANATOLIAN FAULT

Many devastating earthquakes in Turkey occur along the North Anatolian Fault, which arcs from the Sea of Marmara to Lake Van.
(A Closer Look, page 50)

Diverse Climates

Turkey's geographical location suggests that the country's
climate should be temperate, or without extremes. Turkey's
many highlands and mountainous coastlands, however, give
the country a climate that varies from region to region, even
during the same season. The coastal regions in western Turkey
experience the country's longest summers and mildest winters.
In the city of Istanbul, for example, the average winter
temperature is 43° Fahrenheit (6° Celsius), while the average
summer temperature is 75° F (24° C). On the Anatolian Plateau,
the difference between summer and winter temperatures is more
extreme. In Ankara, the country's capital, winters dip to an icy
26° F (-3° C), while summers reach 86° F (30° C). Mountainous
eastern Turkey has the harshest climate. Summer in this region
is extremely hot and dry, while winter is bitterly cold. The
average summer temperature is always well above 86° F (30° C),
reaching 100° F (38° C) on some days, while the average winter
temperature often falls below 23° F (-5° C).

Above: **The owners of
these souvenir shops
near the city of
Pamukkale do not
allow chilly weather
to disturb business.**

**THE REGION WITH
THE MOST RAIN**

Facing the Black Sea,
the northeastern
coastland of Turkey is
the country's wettest
region. The area is rainy
throughout the year,
receiving up to 95 inches
(240 centimeters) of
rainfall every year — four
to six times the amount
of rain other parts of
Turkey receive.

Plants and Animals

Turkey has a diverse range of plant life that covers the country's thick forests, fertile river valleys, and vast grasslands, or steppes. Steppes occur in central and eastern Anatolia, southeastern Turkey, and Thrace — the area north and northwest of the Sea of Marmara. Forests grow throughout the rest of the country, mainly along the Black, Mediterranean, and Aegean seas. The western and middle Taurus Mountains also have thick forests. Much more of Turkey's land area used to be covered with forest, but decades of logging have left the country relatively bare. The Turkish government today encourages conservation and reforestation.

Turkey and other countries in the Balkan Peninsula have similar wild animal populations, which include bears, deer, jackals, foxes, wolves, and leopards. Wild boars thrive in the Turkish forests, where they are seldom hunted. Most Turks, being Muslim, are bound by their religion to avoid contact with boars. Camels, water buffaloes, and Angora goats are domesticated animals in Turkey. Migrating birds, such as eagles, hawks, and falcons, fly over the Bosporus each year. Mackerel, bonito, and bluefish are abundant in the Turkish Straits, while anchovies are plentiful in the Black Sea.

SOIL EROSION

Turkey suffers from several environmental problems, including water and air pollution and soil erosion.
(A Closer Look, page 66)

Below: **Centuries of indiscriminate logging have resulted in thinning forests in northeastern Turkey.**

History

Ancient Anatolia

Before the Republic of Turkey was created, the region was known as Anatolia, an area defined by the Black Sea, the Sea of Marmara, the Aegean and the Mediterranean Seas, and the southeastern Taurus Mountains. Nearby islands in the Aegean Sea were also considered part of Anatolia. The first known people to live in Anatolia settled at Hacilar, a site near Lake Egridir. Evidence of human existence unearthed at Hacilar dates back to a period between 8000 and 9000 B.C. Çatalhüyük, which is near the city of Konya, is Anatolia's second oldest settlement, with relics dating back to between 7000 and 7500 B.C.

The first major civilization in Anatolia was established by the Hittites about 1900 B.C. Very little is known about their origins, except that they entered Anatolia from the northeast. The Hittites rose to power by gradually uniting the native Anatolian communities. Hittite rule, which covered mainly central and eastern Anatolia, as well as the northern regions of Syria, came to an end about 1200 B.C.

Opposite: **The ruins of this ancient Ephesian palace lie just south of the city of Izmir. Ephesus was an ancient Greek city where early Christian communities lived.**

Below: **About 124 miles (200 km) east of Ankara, a roadside stall sells souvenir copies of Hittite drawings outside what was once the Hittite capital of Hattusas.**

Persian, Byzantine, and Seljuk Empires

Following the end of Hittite rule, Anatolia was dominated by a series of different tribes, the last of which were the Lydians. In 546 B.C., Anatolia became part of the massive Persian Empire. The Persians, however, lost Anatolia to the Macedonians in a conquest led by Alexander the Great (356–323 B.C.) in 334 B.C.

In 133 B.C., the Romans gained control over western Anatolia. They also gradually conquered the rest of Anatolia in the course of the second and first centuries B.C. By A.D. 395, the Roman Empire was divided. The western half fell in A.D. 476, but the eastern half, including Anatolia, flourished as the Byzantine Empire. Under Roman rule, Anatolia was largely peaceful, and Christianity spread throughout the land.

Although the Byzantine Empire officially ended in 1453 with the fall of Constantinople (now Istanbul), unrest began in the mid-1000s, when the Seljuks, a tribe of Turkish warriors, took control of central and eastern Anatolia. The Seljuk Empire fell to the Mongols in 1243, but the influence of the Seljuk Turks remained strong in Anatolia.

THE HOLY WARS

The Seljuk Turks conquered Armenia, Palestine (now part of Israel), and most of Iran before invading Anatolia in 1071. They brought Islam and the Turkish language to Anatolia. European Christians were deeply troubled by what they saw as a uniform Muslim invasion of Christian territories, and they organized a series of wars against the Muslims called the Crusades (1095–1270).

The Ottoman Empire

During the 1330s, a group of Turks called the Ottomans founded a principality in northwestern Anatolia near what is now Bursa. The Ottomans rapidly expanded their control of Anatolia. By 1345, all that remained of the Byzantine Empire was the area around Constantinople (now Istanbul), which the Ottomans took in 1453. By 1481, the Ottoman Empire included much of eastern Europe and the Middle East, as well as parts of northern Africa.

In the sixteenth century, the Ottoman Empire continued to expand, but the fabric of the Ottoman society had begun to fray. Among the growing number of problems at that time were overpopulation, unemployment, and religious riots. The economy also suffered when Ottoman-controlled trade routes were taken over by Russia. During the 350 years the Ottoman Empire took to grind to a halt, several rulers attempted social reform, but the ailing empire never fully recovered. World War I (1914–1918) dealt a crushing, final blow to the Ottomans, who fought on the side of the Germans.

Mustafa Kemal Atatürk (1881–1938)

In 1919, the Allies (principally Great Britain, France, Greece, and Russia) began dividing up the Ottoman Empire among themselves. The Turks deeply resented their government for not resisting the Allies and organized a nationalist movement under the leadership of Mustafa Kemal, a military hero. When the Ottoman ruler agreed to give the major portion of Anatolia to the Allies, the nationalist forces drove the Allies out of the country and abolished the Ottoman government. A peace treaty signed in 1923 set the borders of the country about where they are today.

Modern Turkey was founded on October 29, 1923, with Ankara as the capital city. Turkish society underwent major changes under Kemal, who became the country's first president and prime minister. He implemented sweeping reforms to secularize as well as westernize Turkey. In 1928, following a decision by Kemal's government, Islam ceased to be the state religion. Muslim Turks were bound by civil rather than religious marriages. Turks were also banned from wearing religious garments outside places of worship. In the Turkish language, the Roman alphabet replaced the Arabic equivalent, and surnames, which Turks did not have previously, were adopted.

Above: Mustafa Kemal's lifetime of excellence is reflected in his full name. Born in Greece, he was first named Mustafa by his parents. Mustafa was later nicknamed *Kemal*, which means "the perfect one," for his flawless performance in mathematics. In 1934, when Turks were required by law to have surnames, the Turkish Grand National Assembly, the Turkish parliament, honored Kemal with the surname *Atatürk*, which means "Father of Turks."

GALLIPOLI

Many people around the world remember Gallipoli as the site of a mass grave for thousands of young men who fought in World War I.
(A Closer Look, page 56)

Opposite: This drawing is an artist's impression of the day the Byzantine capital, Constantinople, fell to the Ottomans.

13

After World War II

During and after World War II (1939–1945), Turkey sided with the democratic Western nations. The country sought protection against the Soviet Union from the United States. The Truman Doctrine of 1947 provided economic and military aid to any country threatened by communism.

Democratic rule in Turkey continued until 1960, when the Turkish military seized control. Over the following twenty years, the government changed hands many times, alternately ruled by military and civilian forces. During these years, Turkey and Greece nearly went to war over the island of Cyprus, which both claimed. Fighting broke out twice in the 1960s. A settlement was arranged in 1974 by outside forces, and Cyprus became an independent republic in 1983.

In 1983, Turkey returned to civilian rule. Through the end of the twentieth century, the government of Turkey was both democratic and secular.

CYPRUS: A COUNTRY DIVIDED

Turkey and Greece share a volatile political relationship that began several centuries ago. Today, conflicts between the two center on Cyprus.
(*A Closer Look, page 48*)

Süleyman the Magnificent (1494–1566)

The Ottoman Empire had reached its height when Süleyman I, or Süleyman the Magnificent, was crowned in 1520. Selim I, Süleyman's father, had doubled the size of the empire during his rule, adding Syria and Palestine, as well as the northern parts of Egypt, Libya, and Algeria. During Süleyman's forty-six-year rule, the Ottoman Empire dominated the northern and southern coastlands of both the Black and Mediterranean Seas. Süleyman I lifted Ottoman civilization to an unprecedented high, encouraging the growth of art, architecture, and literature, as well as establishing a system of law. In fact, the Europeans of that era coined the nickname "the Magnificent." The Turks called him "the Lawgiver."

Süleyman I

Tansu Çiller (1946–)

In 1993, Tansu Çiller became Turkey's first female prime minister. An expert economist, Çiller studied at the Bogazici University of Istanbul and then at the University of Connecticut, where she ultimately earned a doctorate. In 1991, Çiller entered politics as a member of parliament representing the True Path Party. Her election as prime minister in 1993 was applauded by the West, which saw Çiller's Western education and commitment to economic liberalization as beneficial to Turkey's political and economic progress. Çiller privatized much of Turkey's government-controlled enterprises. Çiller's government, however, eventually fell apart due to internal squabbling and the growing strength of the Islamic party. She stepped down in 1996.

Tansu Çiller

Ahmet Necdet Sezer (1941–)

Ahmet Necdet Sezer became the tenth president of Turkey on May 16, 2000. Before becoming president, Sezer was the country's top judge for two years. Sezer is the fourth civilian to become president. Turkey's other presidents were from either military or political backgrounds. Sezer is an outspoken advocate of democracy and human rights in Turkey, especially in the areas of law and politics. He has pledged to curb the trend of Islamic values and practices encroaching on Turkish politics since the 1980s.

Ahmet Necdet Sezer

Government and the Economy

Parliament

The Turkish system of government is officially identified as a republican parliamentary democracy. The Turkish Grand National Assembly (TGNA) is the country's parliament, elected by Turkish citizens over the age of eighteen. The TGNA consists of 550 members, and each member serves a five-year term.

The TGNA elects the Turkish president, who serves a seven-year term. The president appoints the prime minister, who then selects the members of the Council of Ministers. The president must approve and appoint the ministers, who make up the Turkish equivalent of a cabinet.

The Turkish prime minister is almost always the leader of the political party that has the highest number of seats in the TGNA. Since the 1960s, many political parties, especially the smaller ones, have taken to forming coalition governments in order to gain a majority status. Until 1946, only one political party ruled the government, but today over twenty political parties represent the interests of the Turkish people, including the Democratic Left Party, the True Path Party, the Motherland Party, and the Nationalist Action Party.

Left: **This guarded driveway leads to Turkey's Parliament House in Ankara.**

Local Government and the Military

Turkey officially has eighty provinces, and an eighty-first province is awaiting validation. Each province is divided further into districts and subdistricts. Turkish provinces are supervised by governors appointed by the Council of Ministers. Nominated governors are also subject to the president's approval. In rural Turkey, each village is governed by a village chief, who is assisted by a council of elders. Villagers elect both the chief and the council.

The Turkish Armed Forces consists of the Land Forces, the Navy, the Air Force, the Coast Guard, and the Gendarmerie, or armed police. Unless physically unable, all male Turks between the ages of twenty and forty-nine must perform military service. The compulsory military training lasts for eighteen months. Records suggest that over 11 million Turks were fit for military service in 2000.

Between the 1960s and 1980s, the Turkish military has had to overrule the country's government three times (in 1960, 1971, and 1980). Each instance of military intervention brought on political instability in the country, when democracy and secularism were threatened and violence was rampant.

Above: **Due to severe political unrest in Turkey's past, soldiers are stationed throughout the country to keep the peace.**

Agriculture, Mining, and Manufacturing

Agriculture in Turkey employs about half of the country's work force, at 45.8 percent. Cereals, such as wheat, barley, rice, and corn, are the country's main cash crops. Tobacco and cotton are also cultivated in bulk. On a smaller scale, Turkish farmers produce a wide range of fruits and vegetables, including olives, eggplant, cabbage, sugar beets, potatoes, apples, and grapes.

Turkey is extremely rich in natural resources, exporting large amounts of boron and copper each year. The country is one of the world's largest exporters of chromium ore. Other minerals mined in Turkey include coal, iron ore, lead, sulfur, and zinc. About 24 million barrels of fossil fuel and 20 billion cubic feet (0.5 billion cubic meters) of natural gas are extracted in Turkey each year, providing the country with all its energy needs.

The manufacturing industry in Turkey is dominated by textiles, processed food, petroleum and its by-products, iron, and steel. Turkey's manufacturing sector employs 20.5 percent of the country's work force.

Above: **These women in Edirne are removing the husks from their harvest of corn.**

TRADE PARTNERS

Germany is Turkey's main export partner and bought about one-fifth of all Turkish goods and produce in 1999. Other major buyers are Italy, Russia, the United Kingdom, and the United States. In return, Turkey imports mostly machinery and semi-finished goods from Germany, Italy, France, the United Kingdom, and the United States.

Tourism and the Service Industry

The Turkish service industry accounts for more than half the country's earnings, at 53 percent of the gross national product. Service professions in the banking, financial, telecommunications, and tourism sectors are major contributors to the Turkish economy. Tourism, especially, earns millions of dollars each year from foreign currency exchange, which can be very profitable. For example, out of a workforce of almost 24 million people, fewer than 2 million Turks work abroad (mostly in Germany and Saudi Arabia), and yet their remittances, or the money they send home, amount to 2 to 3 percent of the gross national product.

Turkey draws millions of tourists each year, with its archaeological and historical sites, rare religious architecture, breathtaking geographical formations, and unique East-West fusion culture. In 1998, Turkey hosted about 9 million tourists, who spent approximately U.S. $1.8 billion. It is not surprising, then, that all the major Turkish cities, including Ankara, Istanbul, Bursa, Bodrum, and Gallipoli, as well as some of the smaller ones, unabashedly cater to tourists.

THE GRAND BAZAAR

Bazaars first emerged in Turkish society during Ottoman times. *Bazaar* is the Persian word for market. One of the country's major tourist attractions, the Grand Bazaar in Istanbul is reputedly the largest bazaar in the world, with over four thousand shops packed into sixty streets.

(A Closer Look, page 58)

Below: A group of tourists in Troy, a historical site at the mouth of Dardanelles and near Gallipoli, listens attentively to a tour guide.

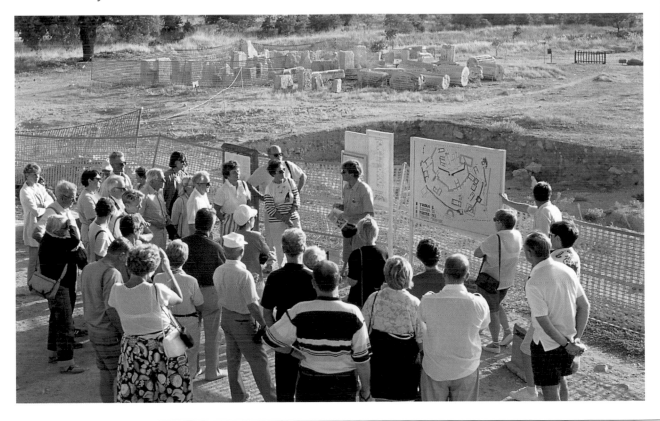

People and Lifestyle

A Diverse Community

Turkey's population is fast approaching 66 million according to population estimates in 2000. Eighty percent of Turks today are descended from the Turkish tribes that, starting in the eleventh century A.D., migrated from Central Asia to Anatolia. The remaining 20 percent of the population consists of various ethnic minorities, including Kurds, Greeks, Armenians, Arabs, and Jews.

The Kurds are the largest minority group in Turkey, making up 15 percent of the population. Unlike Turks, Kurds in Turkey are descendants of native Anatolians. Turkish Kurds not only speak a different language from that of the Turks, they also have different customs and traditions. Turks and Turkish Kurds, however, share the same religion — Sunni Islam.

The number of Armenians, Greeks, and Jews living in Turkey today is difficult to determine because many have adopted Turkish identities over time. Greeks and Armenians make up about 2 to 3 percent of the country's population. A substantial Jewish community resides in Istanbul.

KURDISH PEOPLE IN TURKEY

Shortly after World War I, many ethnic peoples, such as the Kurds, the Greeks, the Armenians, and the Arabs, sought independence from the Ottomans, as well as the formation of their own territories or states. The Turkish Kurds, however, were denied autonomy.

(*A Closer Look*, page 60)

Left: Most Turks today are descendants of nomadic Turkish tribes, such as the Seljuks, who settled in Anatolia over a thousand years ago.

Mixing Modern and Traditional Values

Following Atatürk's call for westernization, Turkey's major cities and western provinces became modern and secular. Conservatism and strict religious customs, however, are still widespread in the country's eastern provinces, especially in the farming communities. The conflicting demands of modernity and tradition have had subtle effects on Turkish society. In cities, for example, traditional values, such as family honor and loyalty, remain strongly influential despite the newfound liberty from religious laws and customs. Also, more and more young Turkish women are choosing to demonstrate their commitment to Islam by dressing conservatively and wearing headdresses.

RURAL TURKEY

Turkish villages, especially those in eastern Turkey, usually produce everything they need. Villagers have little reason to go to large cities. Because of this isolation, villagers often still observe many strict customs regulating how men and women behave in public.
(A Closer Look, page 64)

Under Turkish law, men and women have equal rights, but gender relations on an unofficial level are a source of tension in Turkish society. Turkish families continue to uphold traditional gender roles, where husbands are dominant and wives submissive. Women who attempt to establish themselves as equal to their male partners are likely to meet with some disapproval or resistance. In some rural communities, the social code of behavior forbids men and women who are unrelated to become friends. Figures recorded throughout the 1990s show that few women work outside the home.

Above: Women were once banned from wearing headdresses and men from wearing fezzes, or felt caps with tassels on top, because these articles of clothing are symbols of Islam.

Above: **Today, few Turks maintain a traditional family unit such as this one.**

Family Life

The traditional family unit in Turkey was male-oriented and very large. Three generations lived together, including a married couple; their unmarried daughters; their sons and their wives; their unmarried female grandchildren; and their male grandchildren and their wives. Turkish women became members of their husbands' families when they married. Today, traditional Turkish families are rare, except in eastern Turkey. The modern and more common family unit in Turkey consists of a married couple and their unmarried children. According to 1999 figures, the average number of people per household in Turkey is four.

In Turkey, each member of the family is expected to contribute toward supporting the family. The father, who is regarded as the head of the family, is the main wage-earner. Some mothers work to supplement the family income, while others are homemakers. Grandparents also add to the family income by contributing either some of their pensions or some of the money they gain from renting out property. Older children lessen their parents' financial burden by working part-time to cover at least their own expenses, while younger children help by doing the housework.

GENDER EQUALITY IN TURKEY

When Kemal decreed that the government would no longer be Islamic, the move had far-reaching effects. For the first time, Turkish women were allowed to seek education and run businesses. By 1934, Turkish women had the right to vote, as well as to be members of the Turkish parliament.

Starting a New Family

A traditional Turkish wedding involved the entire family and required months of planning and preparation, which included organizing the ceremony and the wedding feast, as well as assembling musicians and folk dancers to provide the day's entertainment. Today, such elaborate weddings are held only in the rural parts of Turkey. After Turkey became a republic, Turkish marriages that were once primarily religious ceremonies became civil ceremonies.

When a Turkish woman announces her first pregnancy to her family, it is customary for her mother-in-law to give her a gold bracelet after hearing the good news. After the baby is born, the new mother receives more gold jewelry, and her child is showered with many gifts. According to Turkish custom, a woman who has just given birth must be housebound for forty days. Working mothers in Turkey are therefore entitled to forty days of maternity leave with the birth of every child.

TURKISH NAMES

Many Turkish children have names that reflect the time of day or the time of year they were born; for example, *Safak* (sah-FAHK) means "dawn," *Bahar* (bah-HAHR) means "spring," and *Ramazan* (RAH-mah-zahn), or *Ramadan*, refers to the Islamic holy month.

Left: These newlyweds smile for the camera in front of the Blue Mosque in Istanbul. Unlike rural weddings, wedding ceremonies in urban Turkey are usually simple and straightforward affairs.

Education

When Turkey became a republic, all *madrasahs* (mah-DRAH-sahs), or Islamic schools, were closed, and secular schools were established to replace them. A few madrasahs have since reopened, but they are controlled by the government, which closely monitors their curricula.

The Turkish public education system consists of five stages — preschool, elementary school, middle school, high school, and university. Preschool education is for Turkish children between the ages of four and six. Preschool classes are free but not compulsory. Few Turkish parents send their children to preschool.

Turkish elementary school spans five years and is compulsory for all children between the ages of seven and eleven. The country has approximately 46,000 elementary schools providing free education, and they are 97 percent full.

Turkish middle school consists of a three-year course for children aged twelve to fourteen. Although middle school is free and compulsory, the Turkish ministry of education sometimes exempts children living in rural Turkey, where middle schools are few and far between.

LITERACY RATES IN TURKEY

Over 80 percent of Turks aged fifteen and above are literate. The literacy rate for Turkish men (92 percent) is higher than for Turkish women (72 percent).

Below: These elementary students in rural Turkey may not have the chance to continue their education because only a few middle schools exist in the rural areas of Turkey.

Above: **The square in front of the University of Istanbul is always bustling with activity.**

High school is not compulsory but has free tuition. Turkey's 1,300 public high schools are either academic high schools, called *lycées* (lee-SAYS), or vocational schools. The lycées are coeducational and offer college preparatory courses over three years. Vocational schools, on the other hand, span four years and include technical courses in nursing, business, and agriculture.

Turkey has over two hundred institutions offering advanced education. Among the Turkish students who graduate from high school, only 5 percent go on to attend a local university. To qualify for university attendance, students must pass the nationwide university entrance exam. A complicated grading system that only issues passes equal to the number of university places available is used to assess the students. The system gives each passing student a score. Even after a student has passed the entrance exam and qualified for enrollment, there may still be a problem. Only those students with the highest scores are accepted for individual fields of study. Students with poorer results may have to reconsider and alter the fields of study they had initially hoped to pursue.

MAJOR TURKISH UNIVERSITIES

The major Turkish universities are the University of Istanbul, the Aegean University in Izmir, the University of Ankara, and the Middle East Technical University, which is also in Ankara.

ISLAM AND GENDER ROLES

In theory, both men and women should follow the Five Pillars of Islam. In practice, however, men are expected to follow these principles more closely than women. For this reason, women who pray at the mosques usually give up their places for men if the mosques are full during prayer times.

Religion

The vast majority of Turks — 99.8 percent — are Muslims. Turks who belong to other religions, such as Christianity and Judaism, make up only 0.2 percent of the population. Despite the dominance of Islam in the country, however, Turkey is not a theocracy. All matters relating to religion are handled by the Turkish Department of Religious Affairs.

The Islamic faith has five principles, known as the Five Pillars of Islam, that every Muslim should follow. The first principle is the *shahadah* (shah-HAH-dah), which is the declaration of faith a Muslim performs by reciting, "There is no God but Allah and Muhammed is his messenger." The second principle is to practice *salat* (sah-LAHT), or to pray formally to Allah five times a day: at dawn, at noon, in the afternoon, at dusk, and at night. The third principle, *saum* (sah-OHM), involves fasting for thirty days during the Islamic holy month of Ramazan. Outside of Turkey, the Islamic holy month is more commonly known as Ramadan. The fourth principle is that of *zakat* (zeh-KAHT), which involves donating money to the poor and needy. The fifth principle is the *haj* (HAHGE), which is a yearly pilgrimage Muslims around the world make to the Islamic holy city of Mecca, in Saudi Arabia.

THE WHIRLING DERVISHES

Süfism is a mystical form of Islam. In Turkey, some Süfis belong to a group called Members of the Order of Dervishes.
(*A Closer Look, page 72*)

The Turkish government has been secular for many decades. Laws are in place against involving religion in politics and against public preaching, but the constitution guarantees religious freedom. Mosques are maintained by the government, which also issues licenses to Muslim religious leaders and provides religious education in public schools. The Islamic faith has two major types of followers: Sunni and Shi'ite Muslims. More than two-thirds of the Turkish population are Sunni Muslims.

In Turkey, many Muslims tend not to follow strictly the five Islamic principles or observe all the Islamic laws, such as praying five times a day or abstaining from alcohol. For all Muslims, however, Friday is a holy day, when noontime prayers have to be said at the mosque. About one-third of male Turks visit the mosque on Friday for noontime prayers, while almost 80 percent of male Turks visit the mosque for early morning prayers on the first days of *Seker Bayram* (shay-KAIR BYE-rahm) and *Kurban Bayram* (KOR-bahn BYE-rahm), two major religious holidays in Turkey. The Islamic holy book is the Qur'an.

RELIGIOUS HOLIDAYS

Seker Bayram and Kurban Bayram are two major festive seasons in Turkey. Much like Christmas, these two holidays have their roots in religion, but people who are not particularly religious have come to celebrate them as well.
(A Closer Look, page 62)

Below: **The Blue Mosque in Istanbul is a majestic piece of Ottoman architecture. The mosque earned its name from the blue Iznik tiles that cover its interior.**

Language and Literature

The Turkish Language

About 90 to 95 percent of the Turkish population speaks Turkish. The remaining 5 to 10 percent, who usually come from different ethnic backgrounds, speak their mother tongues, such as Kurdish, Arabic, Armenian, or Greek. Turkish is a member of the Altaic family of languages, which were originally spoken by the peoples native to the Altai Mountains, a mountain range in Central Asia. The migrating Seljuk tribes first introduced Turkish to the Anatolian region in the eleventh century. When the Ottomans came to power, they injected Arabic elements into the language, which developed into Ottoman Turkish, or *Osmanli* (ohs-MAHN-lee). Osmanli prevailed for over six hundred years until Atatürk westernized the language at the beginning of the twentieth century. He not only replaced the Arabic alphabet with the Roman equivalent, but he also reformed the rules of Turkish grammar. Modern Turkish is a systematic and expressive language.

Left: **A resident of Kars, in eastern Turkey, is keeping up with the latest news while relaxing outdoors.**

Turkish Authors

Traditional Turkish literature dealt with religious themes and life under Ottoman rule, while modern literature tends to focus on issues of nationalism and social justice. Famous modern authors include Yasar Kemal (1923–) and Orhan Pamuk (1952–).

Born in southern Turkey, Yasar Kemal wrote his first story in 1947. His first book, *Yellow Heat*, which is a compilation of short stories, was published in 1952. He then wrote *Ince Memed*, or *Memed, My Hawk*, which won a Turkish literary award in 1956. *Ince Memed* once outsold all other books in Turkey. Today, it is published in more than thirty countries.

Orhan Pamuk's first novel, *Cevdet Bey ve Ogullari*, won the top prize in a Milliyet Press contest in 1979, as well as the Orhan Kemal prize in 1983. His landmark novel *Kara Kitap*, or *Black Book*, is one of the most controversial in Turkish literature. The book was published in 1990 and remains popular to this day. His most recent novel, *Yeni Hayat*, was a bestseller in 1995. Pamuk's books are published in thirteen different languages.

Above: **Most Turks love a good story, which is why they are avid readers. Storytelling plays a large part in Turkish culture.**

Arts

Music

Many types of traditional Turkish music exist, including classical Turkish music, Ottoman military music, and Turkish folk ballads. Each type of music represents a distinct part of Turkish history and culture.

Classical Turkish music uses sounds that are radically different from the conventional notes that most contemporary melodies use. As a result, classical Turkish music may seem discordant or "flat" to a listener hearing it for the first time.

Ottoman military music was originally heard as part of the sound of battle. The Ottoman military bands played clarinets, cymbals, and drums loudly in an attempt to drown out cannon blasts and clashing weapons as the Ottoman soldiers battled.

Çiftetelli (CHIF-tah-tell-ee), or belly dancing music, is another kind of Turkish music. The tunes are lively and often include the sounds of drums and cymbals. In Turkey, belly dances are performed at most festive occasions, such as parties and weddings. Belly dances are also frequently performed in restaurants and hotels as part of the country's booming tourism industry.

Crafts

Traditional Turkish handicrafts include baskets, carpets, embroidered fabrics, pottery, and musical instruments, as well as wooden and stone carvings. In rural Turkey, women still make lace by hand, using the same methods their ancestors used several centuries ago. Most of these handicrafts can be found under one roof, inside any one of Turkey's many bazaars. Turkish bazaars are fascinating places, featuring a dazzling array of goods that range from donkey's milk to furniture to jewelry. Turkish bazaars usually consist of several buildings that are linked to one another by sheltered walkways, creating a bewildering maze of shops. Tourists who visit Turkey are not likely to leave the country without an "evil eye" charm, a popular souvenir. The charm, which is blue and white in color, is believed to protect its owner from harm and is usually made of glass or ceramic. The Turks themselves believe in the "evil eye" charm, and almost every Turkish household contains at least one charm.

Opposite: **The musician is holding a *kemençe* (kuh-MAHN-chay), a Turkish musical instrument. Similar to a fiddle, the kemençe has a rectangular body and three strings and is played with a bow.**

BLENDING THE SOUNDS OF EAST AND WEST

Turkish music ranges from many traditional forms to commercial or popular Turkish songs produced in the twentieth century.
(A Closer Look, page 45)

Below: **Handmade Turkish slippers are popular souvenirs.**

Shadow-Puppet Theater

Shadow-puppet theater is a large part of Turkish folk culture. This art form features two humorous characters, Karagöz and Hacivat, who contradict each other endlessly. Their frequent disagreements often have been used to disguise or express social and political criticism of the time. Shadow-puppet plays were immensely popular in Turkey until movies were developed in the twentieth century.

Many conflicting legends claim to explain the origins of Karagöz and Hacivat. According to the most popular legend, however, these two characters were mischievous laborers who worked on a building in Bursa for ruler Osman I in 1326. They spent most of their time clowning around, distracting the other laborers from their work. As a result, completion of the building was delayed, and the angered sultan had them executed. The people who knew the two men felt sorry for them and created puppets in their memory. The puppets were used to re-enact their pranks and tell their jokes. From this tradition, Turkish shadow-puppet theater developed. Turkish shadow puppets are usually very colorful and made of camel or calf hides. To stage a shadow-puppet play, a light is placed in front of the puppets to cast enlarged shadows of the puppets onto curtains behind them.

COLORFUL CARPETS

Turkish carpets are entirely handmade, requiring a lot of patience and incredible skill.
(*A Closer Look, page 46*)

Left: Turkish shadow-puppet theater is intelligent as well as entertaining. This art form dates back to Ottoman times.

Architecture

Turkish architecture is characterized by the majestic and strikingly simple buildings that were erected during Ottoman times. Mimar Koca Sinan (1489–1588), whose name means "Great Architect Sinan," is widely regarded as the finest Ottoman architect who ever lived, influencing almost all subsequent Turkish religious and civic architecture. Sinan worked for Süleyman I and built more than 260 buildings in the course of his illustrious career, including seventy-nine mosques, thirty-four palaces, thirty-three public baths, nineteen tombs, fifty-five schools, sixteen poorhouses, seven madrasahs, and twelve inns for caravans. Built with a conscious harmony of the parts to the whole, many of his buildings display clarity and logic, eliminating all repetitive elements. His most celebrated masterpieces are Sehzade Mosque and the Mosque of Süleyman, both in Istanbul, and Selim Mosque in Edirne.

The Mosque of Süleyman, or Süleymaniye Mosque, was built between 1550 and 1557 and was the largest mosque built during the Ottoman Empire. Besides serving as a place of worship, the mosque contains four madrasahs, a large hospital and medical school, a kitchen and dining hall, baths, stables, and shops.

The mosque also contains a cemetery reserved for the great men and women of that era, including Süleyman. Sinan, however, denied himself the privilege of resting there by designing for himself a modest mausoleum nearby.

Above: **The interior of the Mosque of Süleyman, or Süleymaniye Mosque, is stunningly beautiful.**

TOPKAPI PALACE: HOME OF THE SULTANS

Topkapi Palace contains many examples of intricate Ottoman tiling (*above*).
(A Closer Look, page 68)

Leisure and Festivals

The Turks are a sociable people and prefer leisure activities that involve their family and friends. This explains why they favor team sports and communal activities, such as dancing, sharing a meal, or simply gathering at a friend's house. Turks also love going to coffeehouses. For generations, Turks have enjoyed exchanging stories over a hot drink and Turkish sweets.

THE TURKISH BATH

The *hamam* (hah-MAHM), or Turkish bath, is an indulgent way to relax, pampering the body from head to toe.

(*A Closer Look, page 70*)

Coffeehouses

Coffee was probably introduced to Turkey in 1555 by two Syrian traders. Since then, coffee and coffeehouses have become an important part of Turkish lifestyle and culture.

During the Ottoman years, coffeehouses appeared throughout Turkey, and the drink was nicknamed the "milk of chess players and thinkers." Turkish coffeehouses drew people from diverse backgrounds, which, in turn, led to political and social interaction. Turks, especially men, gathered at coffeehouses for a variety of reasons, however. Some Turks preferred to discuss current events, while others sought a game of backgammon. The most popular form of entertainment, however, was storytelling, and by the early 1600s, shadow-puppet theater, a sophisticated form of storytelling, had emerged at the coffeehouses. To this day,

Above: **A group of friends in Erzurum gather outside a village coffeehouse to chat over a hot cup of coffee or tea.**

Turks still enjoy a good story. Good storytellers are never short of an audience in Turkish coffeehouses.

Turkish Coffee and Tea

Turkish coffee, or *kahve* (KAH-vay), is made by boiling finely ground Arabica beans in a container called a *jezve* (JEHZ-vay), producing a brew that is thick but not overpowering. Turkish coffee is heated until it foams, and whole coffee beans, which float to the top when served, are sometimes added. Kahve has six levels of sweetness, ranging from fairly bitter to very sweet. The desired level of sweetness must be indicated when ordering kahve since the sugar is added only during the brewing process. Kahve is customarily served in tiny cups. In some villages, it is a tradition to "read" the remains from coffee cups. After the drink

has been consumed, the cup is turned upside down on the saucer and turned around slowly three times. The resulting pattern on the bottom and sides of the cup is believed to indicate the drinker's fortune.

Above: **Regular customers at this old coffeehouse in the heart of Istanbul are enjoying their afternoon tea.**

Despite the worldwide fame of Turkish coffee, *cay* (CHYE), or tea, is a more popular drink than coffee in Turkey. Cay is served without sugar or milk in small, tulip-shaped glasses. A double boiler, which keeps the tea hot without allowing it to boil, is used to make cay. The tea then remains hot throughout the day without ever becoming bitter.

Sports

Turkey is a nation gripped by soccer fever throughout the year. Hundreds of Turkish soccer teams, ranging from provincial to national league teams, play against one another every week. Stadiums in most of the country's larger cities fill to maximum capacity every time there is a match. Popular national league teams, such as Besiktas, Fenerbahçe, Trabzonspor, and Göztepe, also participate in international soccer tournaments and have produced a number of world-class players. Some of these players have moved overseas to play for other countries, while others relocate only during the off-seasons to play in European leagues. Galatasaray Spor Kulübü, the most famous Turkish soccer team, is the country's best team and is based in Istanbul. Galatasaray won the 1999/2000 Union des Associations Européennes de Football (UEFA) Cup against Arsenal in a heart-stopping penalty shoot-out. The match caused mass hysteria among Turkish soccer fans.

Below: Turkish soccer fans are extremely passionate about the sport, and this passion is often reflected in their rowdy behavior.

Wrestling is Turkey's second most popular sport and the country's national sport. Wrestling has a long history in Turkey as well as in other Turkic nations. In fact, the techniques and tactics used by Turkish wrestlers in the past became the foundation for developing wrestling as an international sporting event. Some modern wrestling techniques are even named after their original Turkish versions, such as the sarma, the turk, the eyerk, and the künde. Yasar Erkan won the country's first Olympic medal in wrestling in the 1936 Olympics, held in Berlin. Today, about thirty clubs in Turkey are involved in freestyle and Greco-Roman wrestling. The country has approximately 230 active coaches, 500 referees, and 4,000 wrestlers. Famous Turkish wrestlers, who are also world champions, include Adali Halil, Celal Atik, and Salih Bora.

Weightlifting is another sport in which Turkey excels. Nicknamed "Pocket Hercules" by the press, Naim Süleymanoglu is an Olympic gold medalist. He stands 5 feet (1.5 m) and weighs 137 pounds (62 kilograms). Süleymanoglu's successor, Halil Mutlu, is nicknamed "Little Dynamo." Both of these athletes represented Turkey in the 2000 Olympics in Sydney.

Above (left): During the 2000 Turkish Cup final, Galatasaray midfielder Ahmet Yildirim attempts to score against the goalkeeper from Antalyaspor, the opposing team.

Above (right): Turkish weightlifter Halil Mutlu lifts 304 pounds (138 kg) to victory at the 2000 Olympics. He weighs a mere 123 pounds (56 kg).

FORTY WRESTLERS

The art of traditional Turkish wrestling, or *kirkpinar* (KURK-pee-nahr), did not disappear when wrestling became an international sport.

(*A Closer Look, page 54*)

National Holidays

The Turkish calendar is marked by a number of religious, secular, and national holidays. National holidays are especially important to Turks because they are unique to the country and because they encourage a sense of patriotism and pride.

Above: **These children are dressed in the Turkish national costume to celebrate National Sovereignty and Children's Day.**

National Sovereignty and Children's Day occurs on April 23. On that day in 1920, Mustafa Kemal Atatürk established the Turkish Grand National Assembly (TGNA) in Ankara and declared the date National Sovereignty Day to mark the country's transition from an Islamic state to a secular state. In 1929, Atatürk included children in the holiday because he wanted to emphasize the importance of children in building the future of the Turkish nation.

Other major national holidays include Victory Day on August 30 and Republic Day on October 29. On August 30, 1922, the Turks, led by Atatürk, won a crucial battle against the Greeks. The victory greatly improved the Turks' chances of winning the Turkish War of Independence and led to a peace treaty with Western nations. On October 29, 1923, TGNA declared Turkey a republic.

Secular Festivals

Turkey also celebrates a number of secular festivals each year. Established in 1973, the Istanbul Foundation for Culture and Arts seeks to promote cultural exchange. Every year, the organization hosts the Istanbul Film Festival in April, the Istanbul Theater Festival in May, and the Istanbul Music Festival in June. All of these festivals feature the works of local and international artists.

One of the more unusual Turkish festivals is the Camel Wrestling Festival, held every January in Selçuk. During winter, which is the mating season for camels, the animals are elaborately decorated with colorful headpieces and saddles and paraded through villages. The camels' owners loudly boast of the prowess and strength of their animals during the parade. Before a camel wrestling match begins, two boisterous bulls and a calf are paraded around an arena to excite and enrage the camels, who then wrestle using their bodies, heads, necks, and legs. The camels' mouths are bound tightly with string so they cannot bite each other during the fight. The winner must make its opponent flee the arena or fall on its side.

Below: **Wrestling camels are featured at the annual Camel Wrestling Festival, held each January in Selçuk.**

Food

Nicknamed the "Bread Basket of the World," Turkey is one of the few countries in the world that produces enough food to feed its citizens and still has some left over to export. Turkish food is diverse and delicious. Breakfast in Turkey usually consists of fresh bread with a variety of spreads, such as jam, honey, or butter. Salty black olives, sliced tomatoes, cucumbers, and cheese are also common breakfast foods eaten with bread. Turkish lunches are usually quite large, while dinners are light. Popular Turkish meals include *pide* (PEE-deh), which is the Turkish equivalent of pizza, and *meze* (meh-ZEH). Meze is a selection of grilled meats and vegetables accompanied by *humus* (HUH-muhs), which is a dip made of chickpeas, and grilled *haloumi* (hah-loo-MEE), a tasty goat cheese.

Turks, generally, enjoy eating meat, especially lamb, which explains the large number of meat recipes in Turkish cooking. One traditional Turkish favorite is *kavurma* (KAH-vor-MAH), small cubes of meat cooked in their own fat and heavily salted. Historically, the salt was meant to preserve the cooked meat for the winter months. *Pastirma* (PAH-stir-MAH) is another method of preserving meat. Salt and spices are added to the meat before it is dried in the sun.

EAT MORE SWEETS!

Turkish meals often end with a dazzling array of sweets and desserts, both traditional and modern. About thirty basic recipes exist for traditional Turkish sweets and desserts.
(A Closer Look, page 52)

Left: **These two men are carving meat to make *döner* (DOH-nuh) kabobs.**

Southeastern Turkey offers the greatest variety of sweet and tasty pastries, an important part of Turkish cuisine. Food in this region, however, is also more spicy than in the rest of the country.

Above: **A Turkish boy examines the wide array of food prepared and offered at a local deli.**

Kabobs

Originally nomadic, the Seljuk Turks had a tradition of cooking meat over open fires. This practice of skewering and grilling meat later developed into what we know today as the kabob, or *kepap* (kuh-PAHP) in Turkish. Different types of kabobs are named according to the way the meat is cooked. Shish kabobs, for example, are made by grilling cubes of skewered meat and vegetables. Döner kabobs involve stacking thick layers of marinated lamb on an upright skewer, which is rotated slowly in front of a vertical grill. As the surface of the tower of meat roasts and cooks, thin slices are shaved off and served with bread and yogurt or humus.

A CLOSER LOOK AT TURKEY

Partly in Europe and partly in Asia, Turkey appropriately shares elements of both the Western and Eastern worlds. With a history dating back thousands of years, Turkey owes much of its rich cultural heritage to an intriguing mixture of Persian, Seljuk, Greek, Roman, and Ottoman influences. The country underwent major modernization after World War I with the radical policies of visionary leader Mustafa Kemal, who aggressively led the country's recovery from Ottoman shambles into a democratic and progressive state.

Opposite: **This harbor along Turkey's Aegean coast used to be a part of Lycia, an ancient country and previously a province in the Roman Empire.**

Many aspects of the Turkish lifestyle, such as visiting the hamam or shopping at bazaars, reflect the Turks' ability to cope with the demands of twentieth-century industrialization without relinquishing their traditions and customs. Turks have preserved traditional trades, such as carpet weaving and making shoes by hand, and they still celebrate ancient sports, such as grease wrestling and camel wrestling. Yet the people also enjoy fast-paced, modern Istanbul and the upbeat sounds of contemporary music. They are also taking steps to reforest their lands and settle volatile, long-standing political issues with the disenfranchised Kurdish peoples.

Above: **These women in rural central Turkey are picking cotton. Agriculture is a major contributor to the country's economy.**

Blending the Sounds of East and West

Turkey has a rich history of music, with styles as diverse as classical Turkish, Ottoman military, arabesque, folk, and contemporary popular music. Despite being radically different from one another, all styles of Turkish music are flamboyant, and Turkish singers are the most prominent celebrities in the country, favored over local film or television stars.

In Turkey, traditional folk music is commonly performed live, while arabesque music is often heard on the radio. The latter is very popular in Turkey, and the most famous arabesque singer is Ibrahim Tatlises. Born in 1954, Tatlises was a blacksmith, a construction worker, and a peddler before he became famous. He released his first album, *Ayaginda Kundura*, in 1978, and it broke sales records at that time. His latest album, *Selam Olsun*, sold over 1.5 million copies.

Contemporary popular Turkish music is especially unique, combining Western-style lyrics with the sounds of Eastern instruments, and a modern techno beat. One of the most famous pop stars in Turkey is Tarkan Tevetoglu, who has been called the "Ricky Martin of the Middle East." Tarkan was born in Germany but moved to Turkey with his family when he was fourteen. He began his classical musical education at the renowned Karamürsel Conservatory and was instructed by many famous Turkish musicians. After graduating, Tarkan worked in Istanbul as a salesperson and sang at weddings, bars, and clubs before his break came in 1993. Tarkan's first two albums, *Yine Sensiz* (*Without You Again*) and *Aacayipsin* (*You Are Wonderful*), respectively, made him a megastar in the Turkish pop music scene. In 1997, he released his third album, *Ölürüm Sana* (*I'm Crazy About You*), which sold over 3 million copies in Turkey. Tarkan also went on tour in 1997, performing in London, Paris, and Berlin. His most recent album, which is self-titled, was released in 1999. *Tarkan* is a compilation of his best songs and includes two songs written by the queen of Turkish pop music, Sezen Aksu — "Sımarık," or "Spoiled Girl," which is also commonly known as "The Kiss Song;" and "Sıkıdım," or "Dirty Dancing: Is This All Yours?"

Above: Tarkan Tevetoglu moved to the United States in 1994. Reports stated that he was unable to cope with the Turkish media constantly invading his privacy.

Opposite: Musicians dressed in traditional Ottoman costumes perform outside the Military Museum in Istanbul.

Colorful Carpets

The large number of nomadic Seljuk Turks who eventually settled in Anatolia in the tenth and eleventh centuries brought with them the art of carpet weaving. Early carpets were made with only a few colors and had rough floral or geometrical designs. Such rugs were typically woven on portable looms, which limited the size of a carpet as well as the tightness of its weave. In those days, utility and function were valued over aesthetics. Carpets, for example, were used as blankets, room dividers, or decorative wall hangings.

Carpets produced in Anatolia between the thirteenth and fifteenth centuries are readily distinguished by their vivid colors as well as by their central motifs, which tend to be dominated by stars, polygons, or stylized Arabic writing.

During the Ottoman years, the art of carpet weaving was further developed, with the establishment of the first imperial carpet workshop in Hereke. The factory produced unusually large carpets of exceptional quality. These exquisite rugs not only decorated the Ottoman palaces, they were also used as lavish gifts for the royalty and statesmen of European countries.

Above: **The traditional Turkish carpet is painstakingly detailed and also very durable. Fragments of the oldest carpet ever found in Turkey date back to the thirteenth century.**

Left: **The colored yarns used to weave traditional Turkish carpets are dyed with natural materials. Color is extracted from different parts of certain plants, such as their roots, flowers, or leaves.**

Above: **A handwoven carpet takes months of hard work to produce.**

By the sixteenth century, the designs on Turkish carpets had become more sophisticated and included animal motifs and complex geometrical patterns. During this era, Bergama and the province of Usak, both in western Anatolia, were the two key carpet-weaving centers.

After the sixteenth century, Turkish rugs incorporated lively and intricate Persian designs, which included clouds or feathery, white leaves against backgrounds of pale rose, blue, or emerald green. The Turkish carpets produced during this period were designed mostly for mosques and noble residences. Such carpets are called "classical Ottoman" or "palace" carpets because they were designed by imperial artists and then woven according to the design at the carpet-weaving centers, an unprecedented practice at that time.

By the eighteenth century, eight new carpet-weaving centers, including one at Çanakkale, had been established. Since the beginning of the nineteenth century, carpets produced in Hereke also gained worldwide recognition. Today, the silk carpets woven in Hereke still live up to their reputation of being the world's best.

Cyprus: A Country Divided

Known for its eternal sunshine, gorgeous beaches, and generous hospitality, Cyprus is the third-largest island in the Mediterranean. Since 1974, the island has been divided between its Greek-speaking and Turkish-speaking communities. International powers regard "The Cyprus Problem" as an issue crucial to the political stability of the region.

Most Turkish-speaking Cypriots are descendants of the Ottoman Turks who occupied the island from 1571 until 1878, when the island became a British colony. Greek-speaking residents have inhabited Cyprus for centuries longer. Although Turkey and Greece had an uneasy relationship for most of the twentieth century, their communities on Cyprus lived together in relative harmony for more than four centuries. After World War II (1939–1945), however, Greek plans for expansion sparked a Greek Cypriot movement for union with Greece. In 1960, the Republic

Below: **This harbor is located in the Turkish section of Cyprus, which lies just south of Turkey. The capital of Cyprus is Nicosia.**

of Cyprus was formed. The new nation's constitution gave the Greeks majority representation in the House of Representatives, at 70 percent — an arrangement that satisfied neither Greek nor Turkish Cypriots.

In 1974, when Greek Cypriot forces that supported a union with mainland Greece threatened to take control of the government, troops from the Turkish mainland invaded Cyprus and established an independent state in the northern part of the island. Named the Turkish Republic of Northern Cyprus in 1983, this state remains unrecognized by all countries except Turkey. Since 1974, the international community has spent billions of dollars to keep peace on Cyprus and to reunite its people. Many political analysts believe that a union between northern Cyprus and Turkey would lead to a war between Turkey and Greece because Greece is bound to the Greek Cypriots by a mutual defense treaty.

The peacekeeping movement has succeeded, but all attempts to reconcile the two sides have reached a stalemate. In 1999, about 35,000 Turkish troops were still stationed in the Turkish-controlled part of Cyprus.

Earthquakes: The North Anatolian Fault

The majority of earthquakes in Turkey occur along the North Anatolian Fault, a deep crack in Earth's surface. Slowly shifting landmasses on either side of the crack have caused numerous earthquakes throughout Turkish history. In 1999, two massive earthquakes devastated northwestern Turkey, the country's most densely populated region and industrial heartland. More than 18,000 people perished in the disasters.

The Izmit Earthquake and Its Aftershocks

On August 17, an earthquake measuring between 7.4 and 7.8 on the Richter scale hit Turkey. Izmit, an important industrial city in western Turkey, was nearest to the epicenter of the quake. The disaster claimed more than 17,000 lives and injured over 27,000 people. More than 340,000 homes and businesses were damaged.

The disaster was followed by more than 1,300 aftershocks. A second earthquake occurred on November 12. This earthquake measured 7.2 on the Richter scale and badly shook the provinces

Below: **Many victims of the 1999 earthquakes in Turkey lived in makeshift tents for months before beginning the slow road to recovery. The first of two devastating earthquakes lasted just forty-five seconds.**

about 62 miles (100 km) to the east of Izmit. The jolt was felt both in Istanbul and Ankara. The second earthquake killed more than 760 and injured at least 4,948.

Rescue Operations

On the day of the first catastrophe, the Turkish government declared a state of emergency and requested international assistance. Thousands of Turkish and international rescue workers worked against the clock to rescue the estimated tens of thousands of people trapped beneath collapsed buildings. Many were not located in time. From the devastation, however, also came a few stories of courage and hope, including that of the rescue of Yuksel Er, a forty-year-old accountant from Bursa. He had been trapped beneath a heavy door in pitch darkness for more than three days when his cousin located him and alerted the rescue team. Three hours later, Yuksel Er emerged from the rubble to the cheers of a crowd of family, friends, and neighbors.

Eat More Sweets!

An old Turkish saying advises a person to "eat sweetly and speak sweetly." Sweets and desserts have always been an important and distinctive part of Turkish cuisine. Sweets also play an important part in Turkish social functions. In 1539, Süleyman I gave a huge feast to celebrate the circumcision of his two sons. Records show that fifty-three different desserts were offered to his guests, including many differently colored and flavored puddings, a variety of halvahs, and pastries and cakes. There was also a large assortment of jams and compotes, or fruits that have been cooked in syrup.

Today, halvah, a confection made with crushed sesame seeds and honey, is offered as a gift to people who are experiencing major changes in their lives, such as births, weddings, departures, reunions, or graduations.

Above: **A dazzling array of homemade sweets can be found in almost every Turkish market.**

Seasonal Delights

The most common Turkish dessert consists of fresh seasonal fruits — strawberries, cherries, and apricots in spring; peaches, melons, and grapes in summer; figs, pears, apples, plums, and quince in autumn; and bananas and oranges in winter. Seasonal fruits, especially those harvested in autumn and winter, are also frequently made into compotes, jams, or preserves. Tasty preserves include quince marmalade, sour cherry preserve, and rose preserve, which is made from rose petals.

Other Popular Desserts

Turkish pastry shops sell all sorts of delicious treats. The most famous of these is the *sade lokum* (sah-DAY loh-KUM), or Turkish delight, a sugar-dusted sweet made from fruit juice and gelatin. *Baklava* (BAHK-luh-vah), which consists of layers of pastry filled with syrup and ground walnuts or pistachios, is another classic Turkish dessert. Turks also enjoy *kadayif* (kah-dah-IHF), a dessert made from shredded pastry and syrup; and *hanim gobegii* (hah-

Below: **The Turks love fresh seasonal fruits as much as they enjoy confections.**

NIHM goh-BAY-ih) and *sekerpare* (SHAY-kair-PAH-ray), two kinds of very sweet cake. *Lokma* (LOCK-mah), deep-fried lumps of batter served with a special syrup, is another Turkish favorite. Turkish milk desserts include a variety of puddings, ranging from a subtle rosewater dessert to a substantial milk and chicken pudding. If the weather or the occasion calls for a lighter dessert, then the milk may be omitted. The puddings then can be flavored with citrus fruits, such as lemons or oranges. There are about thirty basic recipes for Turkish desserts. With local variations, however, the number becomes enormous.

53

Forty Wrestlers

Glistening wrestlers search relentlessly for their opponents' weaknesses, their muscles straining beneath a sheen of olive oil. For centuries, oiled wrestling has been a large part of Turkish sports culture. Every year, thousands of male Turks meet in the first week of June to wrestle each other at the Kirkpinar Festival, an oil wrestling competition held at Sarayiçi, near Edirne.

In Memory of Two Brave Men

How the Kirkpinar Festival originated is a topic of much debate. According to one popular legend, this unusual sport began in the mid-1300s, when forty brave men led by Süleyman Pasha, son of the second Ottoman sultan, Orhan Gazi, crossed the Dardanelles bent on conquest. In the course of their long march through Thrace, the men wrestled to entertain themselves during their rest stops. One day, two men wrestled for a very long time. Although both men were very tired, neither would admit defeat.

Below: **In grease wrestling, participants must drench themselves with large amounts of olive oil. The oil makes the wrestlers difficult to grasp and ensures that the contest will be based on tactical skill rather than brute force.**

They continued wrestling well into the night and ultimately died from exhaustion. The men's bereaved friends buried them under a fig tree, where forty springs miraculously appeared the next day. The site was named *Kirkpinar*, which means "Forty Springs" in Turkish.

Wrestling for Supremacy

Today, participants of the Kirkpinar Festival gather in the large, grassy field at Sarayiçi. The competition lasts for three days, with continuous matches featuring twenty wrestlers at a time. Few tactical moves are forbidden, and no time limit is enforced; the match continues until one of the wrestlers is pinned down or submits. Dressed in nothing but a pair of leather pants, the wrestlers coat themselves with a standard mixture of olive oil and water provided by the organizers. The goal of each wrestler at Kirkpinar is to win first prize and hold the title of Baspehlivan of Turkey for an entire year. If he can do this three years in a row, he will receive the prized gold belt.

Gallipoli

Across the water from Çanakkale, a slender peninsula forms the northwestern side of the Dardanelles strait. This peninsula is called Gallipoli, or *Gelibolu* (geh-LEE-boh-loo) in Turkish. For about a thousand years, the peninsula has been crucial to Istanbul's security; any navy that could conquer this area near the strait had a good chance of capturing Istanbul, the capital of the Eastern world. In one of the most famous battles of World War I (1914–1918), the Allied fleet failed in its attempt to capture the shores of Gallipoli.

The Slide into War

At the beginning of the twentieth century, the political climate in Europe was extremely tense. Europe was divided into two opposing blocs — Germany and Austria-Hungary were on one side, while Britain, France, and Russia, or the Allies, were on the other. When war seemed likely to break out between the two sides, the Ottoman Empire attempted to join the Allies on the condition that Turkey's borders would be guaranteed. When Britain, France, and Russia refused Turkey's terms, the Ottoman Empire joined Germany and Austria-Hungary. In 1914, two

Below: This drawing is an artist's impression of the legendary battle between the Turkish army and the Australia and New Zealand Army Corps (ANZAC) at Gallipoli. The Turks and the ANZACs clashed on several occasions. Having fortified their defense by covering their trenches, the Turkish troops were confident of winning this particular battle, but they lost because they had not anticipated that the ANZACs would jump down to challenge them hand-to-hand. The Turkish army eventually won at Gallipoli, driving out the Allied forces.

Above: **This cemetery honors the brave soldiers who lost their lives in the battle at Gallipoli.**

German warships bombed Russian harbors on the shores of the Black Sea. The Allied navy counterattacked in the Dardanelles strait. When the Allied forces failed to take control of the strait, they launched a land attack on Turkey in 1915.

The Turkish success at Gallipoli has been attributed partly to bad luck and poor leadership on the Allied side and to the timely arrival of German reinforcements for Turkey. Another crucial element in the Allied defeat was the strong leadership of Turkish Lieutenant-Colonel Mustafa Kemal. Although a relatively minor officer at the time, Kemal guessed the Allied battle plan and withstood the invasion by bitter fighting. More than 55,000 Turkish soldiers died defending Gallipoli.

Remembering the War Heroes

Today, the Gallipoli battlefields are peaceful places covered in scrubby brush, pine forests, and farmers' fields. Nevertheless, the momentous battle fought there still lives in the memories of many children of Turkish and foreign World War I veterans. Every year, families visit the shores of Gallipoli in memory of the heroism and patriotism shown by both sides.

The Grand Bazaar

In Turkey, shopping is generally split between a *bakkal* (BAHK-ahl), a small traditional shop selling everyday provisions, and a bazaar, a traditional version of the modern shopping mall.

A Humble Beginning

The Grand Bazaar in Istanbul is possibly the oldest and definitely the largest of Turkey's many bazaars. This famous market started as a small assembly of shops and stalls that emerged immediately after the capture of Constantinople (modern-day Istanbul) by the Ottomans in 1453. Over time, the small marketplace grew into several sheltered arcades and, later, a maze of streets in which each street focused on one particular trade or product.

Today, the Grand Bazaar consists of several interconnected domed buildings and about sixty streets and passages, housing more than four thousand shops altogether. The complex also includes a number of mosques, police stations, and restaurants, all of which are open daily except on Sundays.

Below: **Whether indoors or outdoors, bazaars are an integral part of Turkish culture.**

Left: The process of bargaining can last for hours. Shop owners use a variety of sales techniques that range from offering tea to their customers to pretending disinterest in an offer. When two bargainers eventually settle on a deal, the selling price is sometimes only one-third of the original asking price!

The shops of the Grand Bazaar are packed so closely together that they almost conceal the alleyways that lead to different parts of the market. Some of these alleyways are so small that an average-sized adult can barely squeeze through. Merchants in the Grand Bazaar sell a wide range of products, including leather goods, sweets, books, jewelry, carpets, cloth, and antiques. As potential customers walk down the narrow streets, salespeople greet them in every doorway, announcing their wares loudly or whispering special prices to those who stop to look.

Dedicated Artisans

Artisans in the Grand Bazaar take pride in their work. Shoemakers, for example, work within an elaborate hierarchy. Under the supervision of a master shoemaker, at least ten people participate in the making of one shoe. Leather workers also work as a team, often crouched inside stuffy workrooms, snipping and joining leather with old sewing machines. Workers in both industries take pride in their trade and are skeptical of modern techniques or machinery that might make it easier or faster.

Kurdish People in Turkey

The Kurds are a distinct Middle Eastern ethnic group with an ancient history. For thousands of years, the Kurdish people have lived in a region they call Kurdistan, which extends across parts of modern-day Iran, Iraq, and Turkey. Today, the Kurds are believed to number between 20 million and 25 million. Population estimates differ greatly among sources because Kurds do not have a recognized state of their own, and experts often disagree on how to identify someone as a Kurd. Some political analysts have also accused the Iranian, Iraqi, and Turkish governments of distorting Kurdish population figures for political reasons.

Today, Turkey is home to an estimated 10 to 20 million Kurdish people. Although almost all of them are Muslims and physically similar to the Turks, Kurds fiercely protect their language, culture, and ethnic identity. In 1978, a Kurdish group formed the Kurdistan Workers' Party (PKK), led by Abdullah

Below: **Kurds are proud of their heritage and openly celebrate their differences in Turkey.**

Above: **Near the border shared by Turkey and Iran, these Kurdish women are preparing an evening meal.**

Öcalan. The party wanted an independent Kurdish state in southeastern Turkey and, in 1984, Kurds launched a terrorist campaign from bases in Iraq. Armed Kurdish fighters attacked Turkish embassies, officials, and ordinary citizens in an effort to force the Turkish government to recognize Kurdish political demands. The Turkish government granted the Kurds limited autonomy in 1991. Fearing that the Kurdish independence movement could tear Turkey apart, however, Turkish authorities sent military troops to suppress Kurdish rebel activity and continued to ban Kurdish political parties. Turkish forces also attacked PKK bases in Iraq. Between 1984 and 1998, an estimated 20,000 to 40,000 people died in clashes between Turkish troops and Kurdish militants and civilians in southeastern Turkey.

The Turkish government today claims that there is no "Kurdish problem." Officially, Kurds are not discriminated against, and they participate fully in Turkey's social, economic, and cultural life. While the government describes its military action as a necessary defense against civil unrest, the Kurdish people point to the government's destruction of Kurdish villages and to atrocities committed on innocent Kurdish civilians.

REBEL LEADER IMPRISONED

In February 1999, Turkish authorities captured Kurdish rebel leader Abdullah Öcalan. After a trial in Turkey under the watchful eyes of the international media, Öcalan was pronounced guilty of leading a fifteen-year guerrilla war and sentenced to death. Turkish judges have since denied his appeal, but his lawyers are still fighting for his release. Öcalan is currently being held on a prison island south of Istanbul.

Religious Holidays

The Turkish calendar is dominated by two important religious holidays — Seker Bayram and Kurban Bayram. Seker Bayram, or the Sugar Festival, is a three-day holiday that immediately follows Ramazan, the Muslim month of fasting. Kurban Bayram, or the Feast of the Sacrifice, begins seventy days after Seker Bayram and lasts for four days. Although not all Turks are religious, both festivals are widely observed. Many Turks make elaborate preparations, including cleaning their houses and shopping for food, gifts, and new clothes.

Seker Bayram

On the first day of Seker Bayram, Turks wake up very early in the morning to wash themselves. They also apply perfume or cologne before putting on new clothes. Most of the men then proceed to the mosques for early morning prayers. When the prayer session is over, the men rejoin their families before paying their parents or

Left: **Dressed to resemble a Turkish emperor, this little boy celebrates the end of Ramazan.**

Above: **These Turks hold a parade to commemorate Kurban Bayram.**

even grandparents a visit. Upon arrival, all visitors must kiss the hands of the eldest family members, who will then treat their visitors to a large array of sweets and other confections. On this day, visitors are likely to meet other members of their extended family, and everyone gathers to chat while feasting on sweets. Those Turks whose parents or grandparents are deceased visit the cemeteries.

Kurban Bayram

Kurban Bayram commemorates Abraham's near sacrifice of his son, Ishmael, on Mount Moriah. Obeying God's command, Abraham took Ishmael up the mountain and was about to kill the boy, when God stopped him. God commended Abraham for his faithfulness and ordered him to sacrifice instead a ram tangled in a nearby bush.

In remembrance of Abraham, the Turkish people sacrifice sheep on the first day of Kurban Bayram. Immediately after the early morning prayers, the head of each household slits a sheep's throat. Family and friends prepare a feast with the sheep, and a portion of the meat is distributed to the needy.

Rural Turkey

More than half of Turkey's population is concentrated in European Turkey and the coastal regions of the Aegean, Black, and Mediterranean seas, as well as the coast of the Sea of Marmara. The rest of the country — its vast interior and southeastern areas — is relatively thinly populated and dominated by rural settlements. An estimated 30,000 villages dot the Turkish countryside, each with an average of 1,000 inhabitants. The tiniest villages, however, consist of just a few households some distance apart.

In a typical village, rectangular flat-roofed houses with courtyards encircle a village center. Farmland surrounds the village, which usually includes a mosque, a school, a coffeehouse, guest rooms, and some small shops. Most houses are made of unbaked brick or stone. Where people can afford them, larger

A TURKISH VILLAGE DIET

Foods most often included in the diets of Turkish village households are flour, bulgur (a cereal prepared by partially boiling and drying whole wheat), cooking oil, preserved fried meat, dried fruit and vegetables, jam, pickles, tomato paste, molasses, and dairy products.

Left: Women in rural Turkey socialize by working and doing household duties together or by gathering at a friend's house to share news. After a long day's work, men meet at the local coffee shop to enjoy drinks together or to play board games.

houses are built with modern building materials, such as brick and cement. Inside their homes, people traditionally sit on rugs or mats spread on the floor. Tables and chairs, which were rare in the past, are becoming more common.

Rural life in Turkey has changed remarkably little over the centuries. The focus of village life is agriculture, and a typical day begins at sunrise or earlier. After breakfast, the family tidies up the home, milks the goats or cows, and takes care of the other animals. Then the children go to school, and the men and women go to the fields to work. Some women may stay at home instead and look after the younger children, but the older women of the village usually take on this responsibility.

Many farmers still use tools of ancient design. Teams of oxen pull light wooden plows. Sowing is traditionally done by hand, and reaping is done with a sickle or scythe. The majority of Anatolian villages produce just enough food for their own communities. Harvested and stored crops see them through winter. Villagers obtain their other needs, such as clothing, from larger settlements in the area.

Above: **Villagers generally lead simple, conservative lives. Men wear traditional cloth caps, shirts, and baggy trousers, while women favor headscarves, blouses, aprons, baggy trousers, and long skirts. On very cold mornings, the villagers wear heavy overcoats made of sheepskin.**

Soil Erosion

Soil erosion is the process by which fertile, exposed layers of soil are washed away by rainfall. More than half of Turkey's land area consists of moderate to steep slopes, making the terrain particularly prone to soil erosion. Environmental experts estimate that the amount of soil lost every year in Turkey alone is equal to the combined annual soil loss in Europe and Australia. Apart from climatic and topographic causes, soil erosion in Turkey also results from human activity, including overgrazing, logging, and the clearing of forests for agricultural land. Soil erosion affects about 78 percent of the country's total land area, especially parts of central, eastern, and southern Anatolia. Erosion results in other environmental problems, such as land degradation, or the wearing down of the land, and the disappearance of native plant species.

Land Degradation

The wearing down of the land has decreased Turkey's agricultural output in recent years. Wheat, corn, rice, rye, and sunflower production have dropped steadily. As pastures have disappeared from overgrazing, meat production has also fallen.

Below: Land degradation in the rural parts of the province of Antalya has led to less vegetation for these cattle to graze on.

The drop in agricultural productivity has prompted many farming families to move to cities in search of alternate jobs, leading to overcrowding and unemployment in urban areas. Land degradation also reduces the number of plant species that an area of land can support. Some five hundred plants native to the Turkish dry lands are in danger of extinction, including twelve species that provide valuable medicines.

Above: **In 1998, TEMA project managers traveled to different villages in Turkey to educate the local people about their cause. They also helped the villagers design new methods that will suit both their farming purposes and their surroundings.**

Protecting the Environment

In 1992, two Turkish businessmen set up the Turkish Foundation for Combating Soil Erosion for Reforestation and the Protection of Natural Habitats (TEMA). The aim of this organization is to raise public consciousness about environmental issues, including soil erosion, deforestation, and land degradation. TEMA organizes and implements projects in rural development, the treatment and recovery of degraded land, and reforestation. The founders of the organization try to educate farmers and other rural dwellers about ecologically friendly agricultural methods, and they encourage government agencies and private organizations to adopt more environmentally sensitive policies.

Topkapi Palace: Home of the Sultans

Topkapi Palace stands on a small point of land, called Seraglio Point, that extends from European Turkey where the Bosporus and the Sea of Marmara meet. The palace consists of a maze of buildings and was once the governing core of the Ottoman Empire. Built by Mehmed the Conqueror in the mid-1400s, the palace walls guard an opulent interior that is lavishly decorated with Ottoman artwork and artifacts.

Following the design of Islamic architecture, the palace consists of several domed buildings surrounded by a series of four courtyards. The first courtyard is the largest, at 22 acres (9 hectares). Guarded by the Imperial Gate, this enormous space used to be where holiday celebrations for the general public took place. Today, it is a parking lot. The second gateway, the Gate of Salutations, leads into what used to be the Harem, or women's quarters. The third gateway, the Gate of Felicity, opens into a courtyard filled with flowers, which leads into the palace. The fourth courtyard once contained a school for training civil servants. Ottoman government officials and their families lived

Left: **Guarded by the Gate of Salutations, also known as the Gate of Peace, the Harem has since been converted into the Topkapi Museum.**

there. The palace was a home and workplace for thousands of people of many different ethnic backgrounds and religions, as well as the empire's most talented artists and craftworkers. Records show that the palace's in-house population peaked at 40,000 in 1640.

Above: The entire palace interior is decorated with intricate Ottoman craftsmanship.

Precious Artifacts

The Topkapi Palace is a reminder of the awesome scope of Ottoman power and is a showcase for Ottoman treasures, including imperial robes worn by the sultans and their families, priceless jewels, and religious and literary manuscripts dating back to medieval times. Other art objects include intricately designed wool and silk carpets, jewel-encrusted ceremonial ornaments, and finely crafted armor and weaponry. The throne used by Süleyman I is another prized item on display. Made in the sixteenth century from ebony and ivory, the throne is adorned with inlaid mother-of-pearl. The beautiful Topkapi dagger has three unusually large emeralds in its handle, as well as two rows of diamonds along either side. The back of the handle is inlaid with mother-of-pearl.

Below: Ottoman treasures include jewel-encrusted imperial weaponry.

The Turkish Bath

The hamam, or Turkish bath, has a rich cultural heritage. The architecture, structure, and function of Turkish baths today reflect elements of Greek, Roman, and Islamic influence that were incorporated at different points in Turkish history. The ancient Greeks regarded their public baths as health centers, while the Romans tended to use baths as social clubs, where people met friends and discussed current affairs. Public baths, even across different cultures, have always been more than just places to wash. These monumental buildings often included gymnasiums,

swimming pools, restaurants, and even reading rooms. Several buildings were large enough to accommodate thousands of people and offered different types of baths — hot-water, cold-water, and hot-air.

In Turkey, the hamam has been an important part of daily life since Roman times. Today, the Turkish hamam retains many of the social functions of its Roman predecessor. Almost every town has at least one hamam, and the most impressive ones are in Istanbul. While many homes in modern Turkey have their own baths, Turks still enjoy visiting public baths.

Above: **The Cagaloglu Hamam in Istanbul is about three hundred years old. Behind its rather simple facade are beautiful chambers designed in elaborate Ottoman style.**

The Hamam Experience

Often built in grand Ottoman style, hamams throughout Turkey are peaceful places in the midst of modern bustling cities. On entering a hamam, bathers find themselves in a hall lined with changing rooms. In an old-fashioned hamam, this would be the most impressive chamber, with a drinking fountain or a marble pool in the center. Since Islamic law forbids men and women from bathing together, some baths assign different days to men and women, while other baths have separate facilities for the sexes. All bathers, however, are expected to change into cotton or silk bathing clothes — waist towels for men and robes for women — before proceeding to a steam chamber, where bathers lie on a

Below: **These two Turkish men are in a hamam steam chamber.**

marble platform in the center of the room. Heated from below, the platform is so warm that bathers immediately break into a sweat. Many people believe this process cleanses the body by forcing open the pores of the skin. The steam bath is followed by a vigorous Turkish massage, which involves a masseur or masseuse wearing gloves made of raw silk or camel hair to rub dirt and dead skin from the bather's entire body. The bather then soaps and rinses before entering the final stage of the hamam experience, which is relaxing with a cup of tea, coffee, or any refreshing drink in a resting room cooled by large propeller fans.

The Whirling Dervishes

Sufism

Sufism, a mystically inclined branch of Islam, emerged in the Islamic world in the late seventh century. Sufis, or followers of Sufism, seek the mystical union of man with God through dancing, music, and fire rituals. Orthodox Muslims believe such rites are heresy.

The Mevlevi Order

In the mid-1200s, well-known Persian Sufi poet and philosopher Mevlana Celaleddin Rumi founded the Mevlevi Order, a group of Sufis who have come to be known as the whirling dervishes. Based in Konya, a city in southern Turkey, members of the Mevlevi order believe they can achieve divine joy as well as a mystical union with God through ecstatic dancing.

Below: **These visitors are admiring the shrine of Celaleddin Rumi.**

Above: **Whirling relentlessly, these dervishes are performing the fifth part of the sema.**

The Mevlana Mausoleum in Konya, which occupies half of the Mevlevi Convent, is where the embalmed body of Celaleddin Rumi rests. The other half is a former monastery, which serves as a museum today. Apart from tourists, many modern-day Sufis from Turkey and its neighboring countries visit the mausoleum to pay homage to Rumi. At the museum, items on display include samples of Rumi's penmanship, as well as the religious apparel used by dervishes of the past, which consists of cone-shaped woolen caps, short white jackets, and flared white skirts.

The Mevlana Festival

Every year, the Mevlana Festival, held in early December, commemorates the founder of the Mevlevi Order, Mevlana Celaleddin Rumi. During this festival, dervishes perform the *sema* (see-MAH), or the whirling dance, for the thousands of people, both local and foreign, who have gathered to experience one of the world's oldest and best preserved religious cultures. There are seven parts to the sema, with the fifth part, the whirling, being the most emphasized. To perform the fifth part, the dervishes turn their right palms toward the sky and their left palms toward the ground. In this stance, they begin to whirl, turning around and around until they appear to go into a trance.

RELATIONS WITH NORTH AMERICA

Early relations between Turkey and North America were limited until the twentieth century. In the early 1920s, some Turkish leaders looked to the United States for support in Turkey's fight for independence. U.S. policy, however, remained largely one of isolationism, or noninvolvement in the political affairs of other countries. As the Soviet Union became more and more powerful, the United States began to recognize the strategic importance of Turkey's geographical location bridging Europe and Asia. By

Opposite: **The competition between the two American cola giants has found its way into even the remote villages of Turkey.**

forging strong ties with Turkey after World War II (1939–1945), the U.S. government hoped to curb the spread of communism across the European and Asian continents.

Over the decades, the friendship between Turkey and North America has grown into one of mutual respect. The United States is one of Turkey's major trading partners. Today, Turkish-American and Turkish-Canadian communities celebrate and maintain their Turkish culture while making significant economic and social contributions toward their adopted homelands.

Above: **Sailing in the Aegean Sea, aircraft carrier USS *Kearsarge* is one-third of the U.S. Navy's Amphibious Ready Group. In June 1999, the group patrolled Turkey's regional waters as part of NATO peacekeeping efforts. Yugoslavia was experiencing civil unrest at that time.**

Turkey and the Cold War

For many historians, the arrival of the U.S. warship *Missouri* in Istanbul in 1946 signaled the start of U.S.-Turkish ties. In 1947, U.S. president Harry S. Truman appealed to Congress to support Greece and Turkey against growing Soviet influence. Congress responded with a total of U.S. $400 million in aid to both countries. From 1948 to 1951, Turkey received further U.S. aid under the Marshall Plan, a program designed to strengthen postwar economies so democracy could survive in several European countries.

The nonviolent hostility between the United States and the Soviet Union over their incompatible systems of government came to be known as the Cold War. The North Atlantic Treaty Organization (NATO) was formed in 1949 to oppose communist forces in Europe. NATO member countries agreed to defend one another from military aggression by other countries. NATO began with twelve member countries, including Belgium, Canada, France, Italy, the United Kingdom, and the United States. After Turkey participated in the Korean War (1950–1953) on the side of U.S.-led forces, the United States helped Turkey join NATO in 1952. By 1999, Greece, Germany, Spain, Hungary, Poland, and the Czech Republic had also become members. Of the current nineteen NATO members, Turkey has the second-largest army after the United States.

Above: In 1947, U.S. president Harry Truman appealed to Congress for economic and military aid to Turkey and Greece. The U.S. policy of helping noncommunist nations, such as Turkey, resist communism became known as the Truman Doctrine.

THE FIRST NATO MEMBERS

The twelve nations that first came together to form NATO were Belgium, Canada, Denmark, Italy, Iceland, Luxembourg, France, the Netherlands, Norway, Portugal, the United Kingdom, and the United States.

Left: Turkey supported the United States in the Korean War. These Turkish soldiers in Korea were marching prisoners of war back to the command post.

Relations after the Cold War

With the dissolution of the Soviet Union in 1991, the Cold War came to an end, but relations between the United States and Turkey remained strong because of other common interests. Both countries were committed to countering the threat posed by weapons of mass destruction in Iran and Iraq. When Iraq took control of Kuwait in 1990, igniting the conflict that became known as the Persian Gulf War, Turkey fully supported the United States, allowing U.S. troops to use military bases in Turkey. The United States also stood ready to defend southeastern Turkey against potential Iraqi missile attacks.

Apart from the Gulf crisis, Turkey and the United States have cooperated on United Nations (U.N.) international peacekeeping missions. In April 1991, Turkish and U.S. troops worked together in Operation Provide Comfort, to help Kurdish refugees who had fled into Turkey from northern Iraq return safely to their homes. At the urging of the United States, Turkey also contributed peacekeeping forces to United Nations missions in Somalia and Bosnia and Herzegovina in the 1990s.

Above: **Despite the delicate political situation in Cyprus, relations between Turkey and the United States are still fairly strong. These soldiers are patrolling the "Green Line," a border between the Greek- and Turkish-dominated parts of Cyprus.**

A Warm Friendship Today

The strong ties between Turkey and the United States were apparent during U.S. president Bill Clinton's visit to Turkey in November 1999. Addressing the General Assembly in Ankara, the president spoke of the history of U.S.-Turkish relations and of lasting U.S. commitment to the leaders and people of Turkey.

Today, Turkish and U.S. troops still work together on U.N. peacekeeping and humanitarian missions. Turkey provides a strong brigade to help secure peace in Kosovo and maintains troops in Bosnia and Herzegovina.

Above: **In November 1999, U.S. president Bill Clinton** *(left)* **and Turkish president Suleyman Demirel** *(right)* **hosted a joint press conference in Ankara to answer questions about Turkey's proposed entry into the European Union.**

Fighting Terrorism

The United States also works with Turkey to promote peace and stability in the Middle East. In recent years, Turkey has been troubled by the terrorist activities of the Kurdistan Workers' Party (PKK), a group that wants to create a separate Kurdish state in southeastern Turkey and parts of neighboring countries. Terrorist groups use violent methods to force governments and communities to recognize certain political demands. In Turkey, the PKK has bombed public places and kidnapped Turkish

Left: **The crew of U.S. tanker plane** *KC-135* **poses in front of its aircraft after landing at a Turkish air base near Adana. They were in Turkey to refuel other U.S. aircraft flying over northern Iraq in 1999.**

diplomats, ordinary citizens, and tourists. The United States supports Turkey's efforts to curb terrorism. As part of this strong security partnership, the U.S. government sells weapons to Turkey and maintains a U.S. military presence there. The Incirlik Air Base located in southeastern Turkey, near the city of Adana, supports both Turkish and U.S. forces.

Above: **American businesses, large and small, have been vying for a piece of the Turkish market ever since the country was declared a "Big Emerging Market."**

Trade and Investment

The United States is one of Turkey's major trading partners. In 1999, Turkey's exports to the United States totaled $2.3 billion, and its imports amounted to $3.2 billion. As of 1999, U.S. private investment in Turkey stood at approximately $2.3 billion, and about 300 U.S. companies were operating in Turkey.

American investment in and trade with Turkey is likely to keep growing. Turkey is one of ten regions in the world identified by the U.S. Department of Commerce as a "Big Emerging Market," and the U.S. Embassy in Ankara works to promote commercial interests in the area.

In Favor of a Larger Europe

The European Union (EU), an organization of most of the countries in western Europe, works to dissolve the political and economic boundaries between its member countries. In the interests of boosting the Turkish economy, improving living standards in the country, and forging stronger pan-European ties, the U.S. government has been urging the EU to accept Turkey as a member. In 1995, the United States helped secure a customs union between Turkey and the EU. Today, Turkey is a candidate for full EU membership.

North Americans in Turkey

Tourism is a growing industry in Turkey, and the country receives many U.S. and Canadian tourists every year. The most popular destinations are Istanbul and the beach cities of Izmir and Antalya. Most North Americans living permanently in Turkey for nonmilitary reasons are businesspeople.

Above: **Many Americans and Canadians visit Bodrum, a beach city in southwestern Turkey, each year.**

VOICE OF AMERICA

As part of the U.S. government's commitment to its citizens in Turkey, the Voice of America (VOA) Turkish Service broadcasts a one-hour show every day. VOA Turkish Service also prepares a fifteen-minute news program daily, which is aired by radio stations connected to VOA.

The U.S. Public Affairs Department

The U.S. Public Affairs Department in Ankara and Istanbul promotes cultural ties with the United States, providing Turkish organizations with information on American politics, economics, and culture. The department also arranges press conferences with U.S. officials and specialists in various fields.

U.S. Disaster Aid

On August 17, 1999, a severe earthquake struck northwestern Turkey, killing thousands and causing widespread destruction. The U.S. National Science Foundation and various Turkish organizations jointly sponsored a team of Turkish and North American specialists to conduct air and land surveillance of the damage. The U.S. Agency for International Development (USAID) sent two search-and-rescue teams, and the U.S. government contributed military and medical personnel and crisis support to help in rescue operations. Less than three months after the disaster, another earthquake struck the same region on November 12, this time killing hundreds. By mid-2000, the U.S. government had contributed an estimated $11 billion in aid to Turkish earthquake victims.

TURKISH FULBRIGHT COMMISSION

The Turkish Fulbright Commission offers scholarships to Turkish citizens who wish to pursue graduate studies in the United States, as well as to lecturers, research scholars, and graduate students from the United States who wish to study in Turkey.

Below: U.S. president Bill Clinton meets earthquake victims during his five-day visit to Izmit after the second earthquake.

Turks in North America

Turkish immigrants arrived in North America in small numbers throughout the twentieth century. They left their homeland for various reasons, usually seeking better education and job opportunities in North America. In 2000, the Turkish Embassy identified approximately 300,000 people of Turkish descent living in the United States. The largest communities live in New York, California, New Jersey, and Florida. Today, the United States and Canada welcome thousands of Turkish students every year. New Turkish immigrants generally identify with established Turkish-American communities, and family ties are strong. Although young Turkish-Americans dress in modern Western styles and speak fluent English, they still observe Turkish traditions and festivals. Turkish-Americans enjoy spending their leisure time visiting friends and family.

Turkish influence on North American culture is rather subtle, as the Turkish community is a minority. Certain Turkish foods and arts, however, have become popular. North Americans have adopted the döner kabob as a fast-food alternative, and many people take belly dancing classes as a fun way to keep fit.

Above: **In California, Turkish-Americans maintain a close-knit community.**

Ahmet Ertegun and Atlantic Records

Born in 1923 in Turkey, Ahmet Ertegun is one of today's most prominent Turkish-Americans. He moved to Washington, D.C. at the age of eleven, when his father became the Turkish ambassador to the United States. During his late teens, Ahmet and his older brother, Nesuhi, developed a passion for jazz and blues. In 1947, Ertegun teamed up with record producer Herb Abramson to form Atlantic Records. Joined by Nesuhi and Jerry Wexler, a music critic and record producer, Ertegun developed Atlantic into North America's leading rhythm and blues label in the 1950s and 1960s. He sold the company in 1967 but remains its co-president. Today, Ertegun is chairman of the American Turkish Society as well as a trustee of various organizations and a founder of the Rock and Roll Hall of Fame and Museum in Cleveland, Ohio. The Blues Foundation, an organization founded in 1980 to promote blues appreciation all over the world, honored Ertegun with a Lifetime Achievement Award in 1998.

THE ATLANTIC SOUND

Atlantic Records was a trendsetter throughout the 1950s and 1960s, with groundbreaking developments in rhythm and blues as well as soul. In the 1970s and 1980s, the company focused on pop and rock, signing stars such as Led Zeppelin, AC/DC, Genesis, INXS, and Phil Collins. More recently, Atlantic Records has produced the artists Tori Amos, Jewel, Matchbox 20, and Stone Temple Pilots. Atlantic operates today as part of the Time-Warner group.

Left: Co-president of Atlantic Records Ahmet Ertegun (*right*) meets blues singer Ray Charles (*left*) backstage at the Blues Foundation's Lifetime Achievement Awards.

The Federation of Turkish American Associations (FTAA)

Consisting of forty organizations in the United States, the FTAA has been responsible for overseeing the welfare and rights of Turks in the United States since 1956. The federation promotes job and business opportunities by referring individuals, both Turkish and non-Turkish, to qualified professionals. The federation also helps Turkish and non-Turkish companies establish business contacts with the Turkish community in the United States and abroad. As part of its efforts to promote Turkish culture to the U.S. public, the FTAA organizes the annual Turkish Culture Festival in New York City. The month-long celebration includes cultural performances, exhibitions, and seminars, and the traditional highlight is the Turkish American Day Parade down Madison Avenue.

The Assembly of Turkish-American Associations (ATAA)

The ATAA consists of fifty-four associations and individuals from the United States, Canada, and Turkey. The association aims to strengthen U.S.-Turkish relations by providing the U.S. Congress with reliable news from Turkey and organizing lectures and business conventions in North America and Turkey.

Left: **The 1999 Turkish Arts and Culture Festival was held in California. Participants wore traditional Turkish costumes and promoted awareness of Turkish music and handicrafts.**

The Federation of Canadian Turkish Associations (FCTA)

The FCTA includes seventeen member organizations in Canada and represents about 50,000 Turkish-Canadians. The association's drama performances and other activities help promote Turkish culture in Canada and encourage Turkish-Canadians to participate in the social and economic life of Canada.

Above: **Members of the Horon Turkish Folk Dance Ensemble participated in the July 4, 2000, parade, held in Monterey, California.**

Celebrating Turkish Culture

Turkish-Americans and Turkish-Canadians enjoy sharing their culture with the wider community. Turkish-Americans living in Arizona, California, Connecticut, Georgia, Florida, Hawaii, Illinois, Massachusetts, Michigan, Missouri, North Carolina, New Jersey, New York, Ohio, Texas, Virginia, and Washington are known to be especially active in their respective states. Turkish-Canadians, however, tend to concentrate their activites in Ontario.

Many North American schools and universities have Turkish student associations that aim to keep Turkish culture alive for young people. These groups meet regularly to socialize and to discuss current political and social issues.

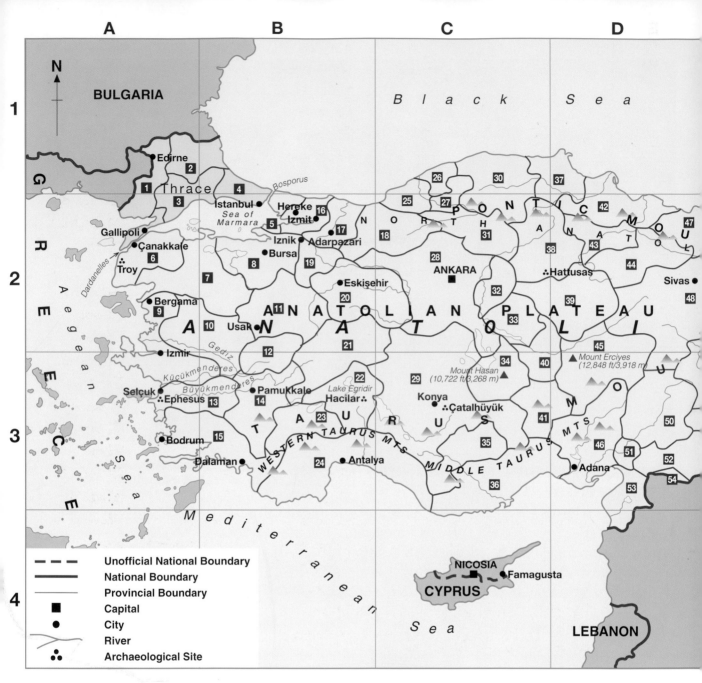

1 Edirne	**28** Ankara	**55** Giresun
2 Kirklareli	**29** Konya	**56** Trabzon
3 Tekirdag	**30** Kastamonu	**57** Gumushane
4 Istanbul	**31** Çankiri	**58** Bayburt
5 Yalova	**32** Kirikkale	**59** Erzincan
6 Çanakkale	**33** Kirsehir	**60** Tunceli
7 Balikesir	**34** Aksaray	**61** Elazig
8 Bursa	**35** Karaman	**62** Adiyaman
9 Izmir	**36** Içel	**63** Sanli Urfa
10 Manisa	**37** Sinop	**64** Rize
11 Kutahya	**38** Çorum	**65** Artvin
12 Usak	**39** Yozgat	**66** Erzurum
13 Aydin	**40** Nevsehir	**67** Bingol
14 Denizli	**41** Nigde	**68** Mus
15 Mugla	**42** Samsun	**69** Diyarbakir
16 Kocaeli	**43** Amasya	**70** Batman
17 Sakarya	**44** Tokat	**71** Mardin
18 Bolu	**45** Kayseri	**72** Ardahan
19 Bilecik	**46** Adana	**73** Kars
20 Eskisehir	**47** Ordu	**74** Igdir
21 Afyon	**48** Sivas	**75** Agri
22 Isparta	**49** Malatya	**76** Bitlis
23 Burdur	**50** Kahraman Maras	**77** Van
24 Antalya	**51** Osmaniye	**78** Siirt
25 Zonguldak	**52** Gazi Antep	**79** Sirnak
26 Bartin	**53** Hatay	**80** Hakkari
27 Karabuk	**54** Kilis	

Lebanon D4

Mediterranean Sea A4–D4
Middle Taurus Mountains
    C3–D3
Mount Ararat F2
Mount Erciyes D3
Mount Hasan C3

Nicosia C4
North Anatolian Fault B2–F2

Pamukkale B3
Pontic Mountains C2–E2

Russia E1–F1

Sea of Marmara A2–B2
Selçuk A3
Sivas D2
Syria D3–E4

Taurus Mountains B3–F3
Thrace (region) A1–B2
Tigris (river) E3–F4
Troy A2

Usak B2

Western Taurus Mountains
    B3–C3

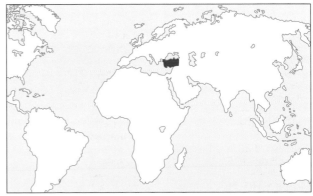

TURKEY

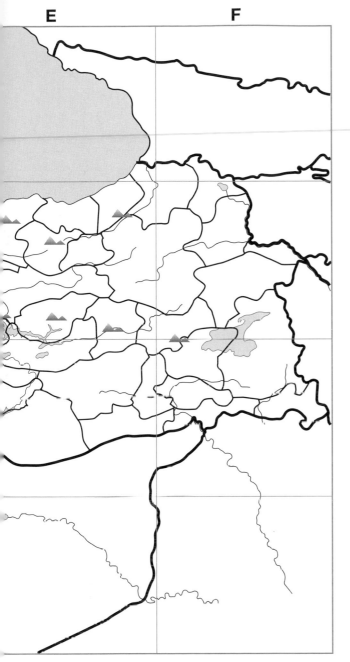

E   F

How Is Your Geography?

Learning to identify the main geographical areas and points of a country can be challenging. Although it may seem difficult at first to memorize the locations and spellings of major cities or the names of mountain ranges, rivers, deserts, lakes, and other prominent physical features, the end result of this effort can be very rewarding. Places you previously did not know existed will suddenly come to life when referred to in world news, whether in newspapers, television reports, or other books and reference sources. This knowledge will make you feel a bit closer to the rest of the world, with its fascinating variety of cultures and physical geography.

Used in a classroom setting, the instructor can make duplicates of this map using a copy machine. (PLEASE DO NOT WRITE IN THIS BOOK!) Students can then fill in any requested information on their individual map copies. Used one-on-one, the student can also make copies of the map on a copy machine and use them as a study tool. The student can practice identifying place names and geographical features on his or her own.

Turkey at a Glance

Official Name   Republic of Turkey (Turkiye Cumhuriyeti)

Capital   Ankara

Official Language   Turkish

Population   66 million (2000 estimate)

Land Area   301,400 square miles (780,626 square kilometers)

Highest Point   Mount Ararat 16,950 feet (5,166 meters)

Major Rivers   Euphrates (776 miles/1249 km)

Tigris (326 miles/525 km)

Major Religion   Islam

Current President   Ahmet Necdet Sezer (1941–)

Provinces   Adana, Adiyaman, Afyon, Agri, Aksaray, Amasya, Ankara, Antalya, Ardahan, Artvin, Aydin, Balikesir, Bartin, Batman, Bayburt, Bilecik, Bingol, Bitlis, Bolu, Burdur, Bursa, Çanakkale, Çankiri, Çorum, Denizli, Diyarbakir, Edirne, Elazig, Erzincan, Erzurum, Eskisehir, Gazi Antep, Giresun, Gumushane, Hakkari, Hatay, Içel, Igdir, Isparta, Istanbul, Izmir, Kahraman Maras, Karabuk, Karaman, Kars, Kastamonu, Kayseri, Kilis, Kirikkale, Kirklareli, Kirsehir, Kocaeli, Konya, Kutahya, Malatya, Manisa, Mardin, Mugla, Mus, Nevsehir, Nigde, Ordu, Osmaniye, Rize, Sakarya, Samsun, Sanli Urfa, Siirt, Sinop, Sirnak, Sivas, Tekirdag, Tokat, Trabzon, Tunceli, Usak, Van, Yalova, Yozgat, Zonguldak (Duzce)

Important Holidays   National Sovereignty and Children's Day (April 23)

Victory Day (August 30)

Republic Day (October 29)

Currency   Turkish Lira (670,130 TL = U.S. $1 as of 2001)

Opposite: **This woman is selling handmade dolls as souvenirs.**

Glossary

Turkish Words

bahar (bah-HAHR): spring.

bakkal (BAHK-ahl): a traditional shop that is stocked with everyday provisions.

baklava (BAHK-luh-vah): a famous Turkish dessert consisting of several layers of sweetened pastry stuffed with ground walnuts or pistachios.

cay (CHYE): Turkish tea.

çiftetelli (CHIF-tah-tell-ee): Turkish belly dancing music.

döner (DOH-nuh): a type of lamb kabob that is skewered and cooked slowly in front of a vertical grill.

Gelibolu (geh-LEE-boh-loo): the Turkish name for Gallipoli.

haj (HAHGE): the fifth of five Islamic principles, which states that all Muslims should make an annual pilgrimage to the Islamic holy city of Mecca.

haloumi (hah-loo-MEE): goat cheese.

hamam (hah-MAHM): Turkish bath.

hanim gobegiii (hah-NIHM goh-BAY-ih): a type of very sweet cake.

humus (HUH-muhs): a popular Turkish dip made of chick peas.

jezve (JEHZ-vay): a special container used to prepare Turkish coffee.

kadayif (kah-dah-IHF): a Turkish sweet made from shredded pastry and syrup.

kahve (KAH-vay): Turkish coffee.

kavurma (KAH-vor-MAH): small cubes of meat that are heavily salted and cooked in their own fat.

kemençe (kuh-MAHN-chay): a violinlike Turkish musical instrument.

kepap (kuh-PAHP): a traditional Turkish dish that involves stacking small pieces of meat and vegetables on a skewer and grilling them over an open fire.

kirkpinar (KURK-pee-nahr): traditional Turkish wrestling; also, forty springs.

Kurban Bayram (KOR-bahn BYE-rahm): the Feast of the Sacrifice.

lokma (LOCK-mah): deep-fried lumps of batter served with a special syrup.

lycées (lee-SAYS): Turkish public academic high schools.

madrasahs (mah-DRAH-sahs): Islamic religious schools.

meze (meh-ZEH): a popular Turkish meal featuring a selection of grilled meats, vegetables, humus, and cheese.

Osmanli (ohs-MAHN-lee): an Arabic version of the Turkish language that developed during the Ottoman years.

pastirma (PAH-stir-MAH): sun-dried meat flavored with salt and spices; a traditional form of preserved meat.

pide (PEE-deh): Turkish pizza.

Ramazan (RAH-mah-zahn): the Islamic holy month, also called Ramadan.

sade lokum (sah-DAY loh-KUM): Turkish Delight, a famous Turkish sweet.

safak (sah-FAHK): dawn.

salat (sah-LAHT): the practice of attending all five sessions of formal prayers held daily at the mosque.

saum (sah-OHM): the Islamic principle that requires fasting for thirty days during Ramazan.

Seker Bayram (shay-KAIR BYE-rahm): the Sugar Festival.

sekerpare (SHAY-kair-PAH-ray): a type of very sweet cake.

sema (see-MAH): the dance of the whirling dervishes.

shahadah (shah-HAH-dah): an Islamic declaration of faith.

zakat (zeh-KAHT): the fourth of five Islamic principles, which says that money should be donated periodically to the poor and needy.

English Vocabulary

advocate: a person who actively supports a cause or person.

aesthetics: a quality of beauty.

arabesque: a fanciful style of Turkish music.

artifacts: objects created by humans who lived in an earlier historical period.

autonomy: the right of self-government.

boisterous: noisy; high-spirited.

coalition: a temporary merger of several parties, or factions.

coeducational: relating to teaching students of both sexes.

compotes: stewed fruit, usually cooked in syrup.

discordant: jarring or disagreeable to the ear.

disenfranchised: without certain basic rights; deprived.

epicenter: a point directly above an earthquake's true center, which is the source of the shock waves.

guerrilla: relating to independent warfare tactics that are characterized by sabotage and radical aggression.

heresy: a religious opinion that is different from an orthodox, accepted church doctrine.

hierarchy: a system of persons or things that ranks one above another.

homage: high regard; respect.

humanitarian: relating to efforts that will improve the quality of life for other, less fortunate, people.

indiscriminate: lacking in care or distinction; haphazard.

motif: a recurring element of design.

nomadic: relating to a lifestyle that involves moving around and that excludes a permanent home.

peninsula: a slender strip of land that extends from the mainland and is almost completely surrounded by water.

principality: territory that traditionally is governed by a prince.

rampant: widespread, allowed to flourish without resistance.

relinquishing: giving up.

secular: not concerned with religion.

stalemate: a situation where no action can be taken or progress made; deadlock.

techno: a style of dance music characterized by very fast beats.

textiles: woven or knit cloth.

theocracy: a form of government in which religious leaders rule, based on divine direction.

topographic: relating to the relief or land formations of a particular area.

unabashedly: shamelessly.

unprecedented: never before known or experienced.

vocational: providing instruction or training in an occupation or trade.

More Books to Read

Daily Life in Ancient and Modern Istanbul. Cities Through Time series. Robert Bator (Lerner Publications)

Iznik: The Pottery of Ottoman Turkey. Nurhan Atasoy, Julian Raby, and Yanni Petsopoulos (Laurence King Publications)

Letters Home from Turkey. Lisa Halvorsen (Blackbirch)

Topkapi Palace: An Illustrated Guide to Its Life and Personalities. Godfrey Goodwin (Al Saqi)

Turkey. Cultures of the World series. Sean Sheehan (Benchmark Books)

Turkey. Festivals of the World series. Maria O'Shea (Gareth Stevens)

Turkey. Major World Nations series. Garry Lyle (Chelsea House Publications)

Turkey: Between East and West. Exploring Cultures of the World series. Louise R. Miller (Benchmark)

Turkey: From the Seljuks to the Ottomans. Henri Stierlin and Chris Miller (TASCHEN America)

Turkish Cooking: A Culinary Journey Through Turkey. Carol Robertson (Frog)

Videos

Going Places: Turkey. (MPI Home Video)

Intrigue in Istanbul. (Discovery Channel)

Splendors of the Ottoman Sultans. (Kulturvideo)

Turkey: Enchanted Land of Cappadocia. (World Almanac Video)

Web Sites

www.smm.org/catal

turktour.com/tips.html

www.cis.udel.edu/~iren/TurkishWorld.html

Due to the dynamic nature of the Internet, some web sites stay current longer than others. To find additional web sites, use a reliable search engine with one or more of the following keywords to help you locate information about Turkey. Keywords: *Ankara, Armenians, Mustafa Kemal Atatürk, Cyprus, Istanbul, Kurds, Ottoman, Seljuk, Turkey, Turkish.*

Index